MULTIHULL
SEAMANSHIP
Illustrated

fernhurst
BOOKS

This edition published 1997 by Fernhurst Books, Duke's Path,
High Street, Arundel, West Sussex, BN18 9AJ, UK
First published in Australia in 1995 by Cyclone Publishers, Mallacoota
3892 Victoria, Australia.

British Library Cataloguing in Publication Data:
A catalogue record for this book is available from the British Library.

ISBN 1 898660 31 X

Acknowledgments
There are no hard and fast rules at sea. Sailing is an art and for this reason
the author would like to thank those who shared their art and assistance
with editing and advice during the production of this book.
Those who helped edit the first edition of this book include:
Lock Crowther (multihull designer)
Ian Johnston and Cathy Hawkins (Verbatim - 40ft trimaran)
Paul Nudd (XL2 - 40 ft catamaran)
Grant Telfer (Orient - 71ft catamaran)
Dean Snow (Trident - 31ft trailer trimaran)
For the Fernhurst edition there have been many who have given advice,
suggestions and ideas. To the Multihull Yacht Club members who
contacted me, the many multihull designers, builders and sailors whose
ideas I have borrowed, tested and adopted; thank you.
My illustrator, Nigel Allison, worked hard and professionally as he put up
with the continuous changes and reviews. Whenever the wind blew he kept
the office cobwebs from appearing by taking me sailing. Thanks Nigel.
Lastly, and most importantly, my thanks to my partner and co-skipper on
land and sea. Without Catherine this book would never have even started
nor would the adventure be continuing.

Edited by Liz Girvan
Text set in 12pt Times New Roman
Printed in Hong Kong through World Print Limited

Foreword

This book is for people who are, or are contemplating, multihull sailing. There are many textbooks on the market which detail general seamanship principles. This is not one of them. This is about catamarans and trimarans and the skills needed to enjoy and understand them to the utmost. Both racing and cruising yachts are catered for, as are trailerable multihulls.

Seamanship is not a black and white skill. It is an evolution of knowledge, a building of information through experiment, thought and experience. There is no definitive word on an evolving skill. Multihull Seamanship Illustrated started as my personal index of 'how to's'. It has grown through experience and by others sharing their knowledge. It is my turn to give some of that back to my colleagues on the ocean who venture forth in hulls of two or more.

Safe multihull sailing.

Dr Gavin LeSueur

Further editions of multihull Seamanship Illustrated are planned. If you have any thoughts, suggestions, criticisms or comments then I would love to hear from you. I can be contacted via the Publisher or at 21-23 Maurice Ave, Mallacoota 3892, Victoria, Australia.
Phone ISD 61 03 51580777 Facsimile ISD 61 03 51580668

CONTENTS

AUTHOR
Dr Gavin LeSueur

Gavin LeSueur built his first multihull, a 16ft Mosquito catamaran, while at high school. After graduating from Melbourne University in Medicine, he purchased and moved aboard a 35' Hedley Nicol 'Wanderer' trimaran. To learn as much about multihull sailing he decided to compete in the two-handed Bicentennial Around Australia Yacht Race. For this adventure he attained the then fastest offshore racing catamaran in Australia - a 37ft Crowther Super Shockwave named D Flawless.

As preparation he raced D Flawless in many Southern Ocean races and eventually to New Zealand in the Two-handed Trans Tasman Challenge. During this 1000 nautical mile race D Flawless, LeSueur and his 21 year old crew Catherine Reed, survived a hammering from Cyclone Bola, sailing though the eye to complete the race and gain the 'best competitors' trophy. En route back to Australia two months later D Flawless struck a whale while surfing downwind at night. The subsequent liferaft story, and his earlier adventures at sea and on land are detailed in LeSueur's first book 'Windswept'.

Within days of rescue Gavin and Catherine were fortunate enough to be offered the use of another catamaran, a Crowther 40ft shorthanded racer named 'John West'.

Aboard John West, Gavin and Catherine competed in the two-handed Around Australia Yacht Race. This marathon, hailed as the toughest coastal race in the world, encompassed more than eight thousand miles of hazards. Swirling tidal currents around tropical reefs in blistering conditions contrasted further down the track with sleet, snow and blinding storms in the notorious roaring forties of the Southern Ocean.

Gavin's story of the Around Australia Race and the drama behind the multihulls that both capsized and survived, is told in his second book, 'The Line'.

Since the Around Australia Race Gavin LeSueur has continued the multihull experience. For exercise he races a Hobie cat whenever the wind blows. Any opportunity to sail aboard the many catamarans and trimarans in Southern Australia is undertaken with enthusiasm. His experience ranges from cruising on the latest trailertri to Three Peaks racing on large offshore Catamarans.

On a personal level LeSueur was once told that if he ever found the perfect crew he should marry them. He did, and with his wife Catherine he had to modify 'John West' before setting off for a years cruising.

Gavin, Catherine and Estelle LeSueur live in Mallacoota, Victoria, Australia. They run an isolated country General Practice in the Croajingalong National Park. Bounded by the quiet waters of Mallacoota Inlet on one side and the notorious Bass Strait and Tasman Sea on the other, the LeSueur family spend their summer months lake sailing and the winter months racing and cruising offshore.

ILLUSTRATOR
Nigel Allison

Nigel Allison is an illustrator, art teacher and a keen multihull sailor. He owns a trailertri, jumps waves on sailboards and races an off-the-beach catamaran. Nigel's sailing background and enthusiastic approach to his art have given the world of multihulls a new dimension. Nigel was able to produce the illustrations for this book with the support of his wife Liz and capable distractions of his two boys, Kai and Leewan. Nigel works full time as an art, music and sailing teacher at Mallacoota P-12 College.

Nigel Allison, Kai, Leewan and Liz

Catherine, Estelle & Gavin LeSueur

ANCHORING

Anchoring a multihull successfully requires the right anchor for the bottom conditions, the correct chain and rode arrangement and burying the anchor effectively.

The classic anchors (e.g. Bruce, Danforth, CQR) come with recommended weights for length yachts. Do not underestimate the required anchor weight because your multihull is lighter than a monohull of equivalent length. Multihulls put a different load on anchors as they sail on the mooring line. In reality most multihulls need about one size bigger than for an equivalent sized monohull. In the traditional anchors this means a heavier anchor. Fortunately there are lightweight, strong holding anchors ideally suited to multihulls e.g. Fortress. These are aluminium, usually more expensive and need to be set well. Their major drawback is that they do not penetrate weed well and do not reset as easily in tide or wind changes.

The features of each anchor type are found in most general seamanship books.

For secure anchoring your yacht should point into the wind and be as stable as possible.

Multihull Seamanship Rule:
Always anchor with a bridle.

The bridle arms should be approximately the beam of the multihull and no longer than the length of the yacht. Always have the ability to play out more scope or take the line in. One way of achieving this is to have the bridle arms

permanently arranged and spliced together into a single line. This single line is then tied to the anchor line with a rolling hitch finished off with a half hitch as illustrated in the Bridle chapter.

Anchoring with a bridle is essential for wing masted multihulls. Lock the wing mast fore and aft where it will act like a normal mast. If the locking device fails to secure the wing mast then any movement will start a mast oscillation. If this occurs the multihull might sail forward and break the anchor free.

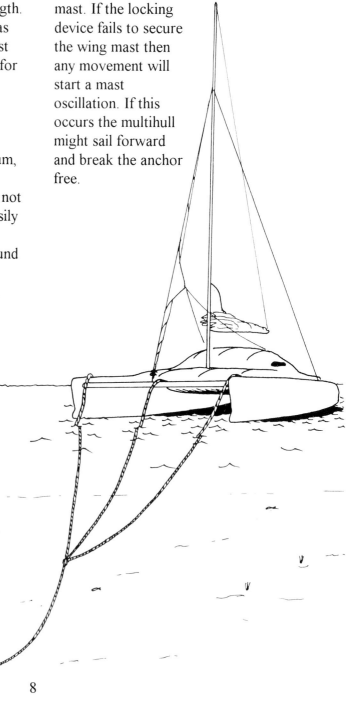

Anchoring problems

Multihulls move more to the wind than to the current and are thus more liable to change the direction that they lay over time. This pulls anchors out and lets them get tangled in the chain, in weed or rocks.

Multihull Seamanship Rule:
If you leave your multihull at anchor always set two anchors diametrically opposed.

This is especially important in areas of strong tidal flow. Best of all avoid anchoring in areas with currents. Monohulls anchored nearby will swing with the current while a multihull may not - creating havoc.

There are numerous anchoring systems to allow for changes in flow or wind direction. A useful one for multihulls is illustrated. This uses the two lines to establish a bridled anchoring setup. The two white ropes are the anchor lines. The black rope is a third piece of line of similar thickness and approximately a metre long.

To tie the bridle knot hold the two anchor lines as one rope and twist them as you would the start of a bowline.

Using the black rope thread it with the following image in mind: The black rope comes up through the loop, around the two white lines on one side, back down the loop and around the two white lines on the other side and then back through the loop.
As with a bowline this knot can always be undone even after it has been subject to very high loads.

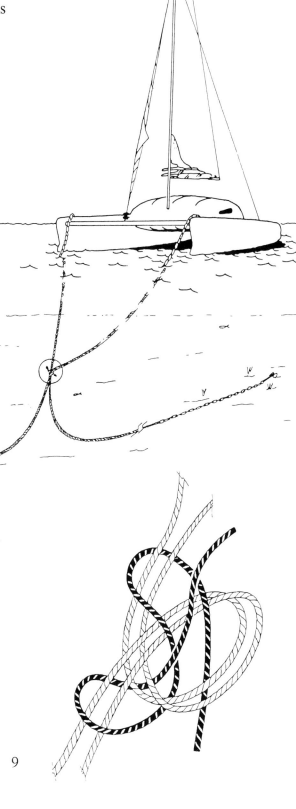

9

How many anchors?

At least two and possibly three anchors should be aboard. Two full anchors for different bottom conditions and a third lightweight anchor for use as a 'kedge'. Fully test each anchor so you know its capabilities before getting caught in a critical situation.

The lightweight anchor can be laid as a kedge to pull the boat off an obstacle if you run aground. It is very difficult to carry a large anchor with chain through a surf line or in a small dinghy. Multihulls are beached easily but are a bit harder to get off if the tide drops. A kedge anchor is extremely useful if you have to leave the beach before the tide rises.

Multihull Seamanship Rule:
Carry a strong lightweight kedge anchor.

Bridle points

Ensure the mooring cleats used for attaching the bridle arms and the central tether tie point are strong enough to take the full weight of the boat. The same rule applies to the strength of the nylon warp or anchor chain. Use an anchor line that has the ability to stretch. If an all chain system is used then at least have some give in the system by using rope bridle arms. The minimum length of anchor line should be five times the depth of the water at high tide.

Because multihulls move on their mooring line you need plenty of effective chafe protection.

If you do not have a bridle system set up, your multihull will sail less on the single line if you set it off centre (from an outer hull). Multihulls with bowsprit spinnaker poles sometimes have a problem turning a single anchor rode into a bridle. This is because the pole supports run to the outer hulls and are in the way. A strong, extendible boathook is often needed to run the lines and retrieve them.

Set up a system that you can use easily. If it is difficult to set up a bridle each time then rethink your anchoring arrangements.

Anchoring under sail

Manoeuvring cruising multihulls under sail is a skill worth practicing . Picking up a mooring buoy is made easy because of the lack of momentum when sails are feathered. Many multihulls will stop in one or two boat lengths.

Sailing onto a mooring

Approach the mooring buoy or area that you intend to anchor on a beam reach. Sail with enough speed to avoid leeway (drifting sideways). Aim about a boat length under the buoy. At the last moment round the boat up into the wind while releasing all sheets.

Drop anchor or grab the mooring and secure it while the headsail is dropped. Drop the mainsail next. Ensure sheets and halyards will run free or you will start sailing as soon as drift occurs sideways.
Secure sails to reduce windage and then set your bridle.

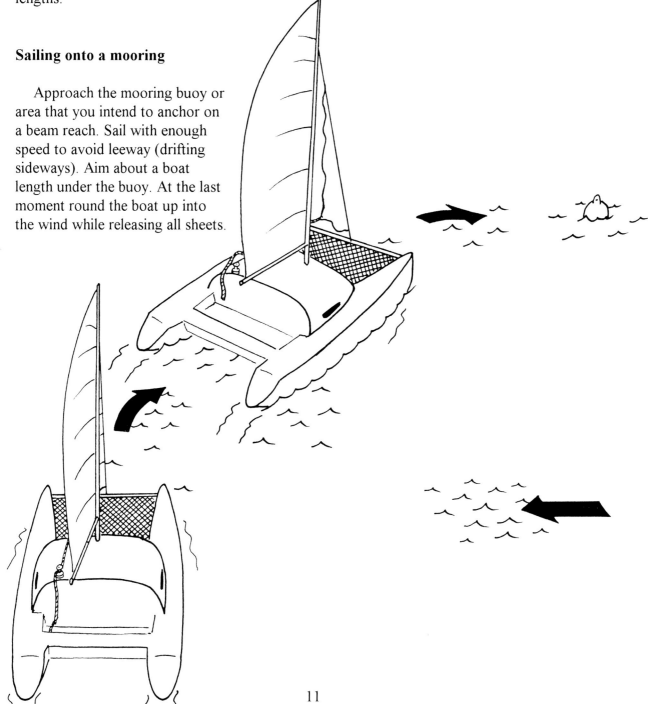

11

Sailing off a mooring

Multihulls are readily sailed off their mooring. Raise the mainsail first but leave the traveller and sheets slackened off. Determine which tack you want to sail onto and reverse the helm so that when the boat drifts backwards it will turn in the desired direction. Hoist or unroll the jib and sheet it on the wrong side for the desired tack.

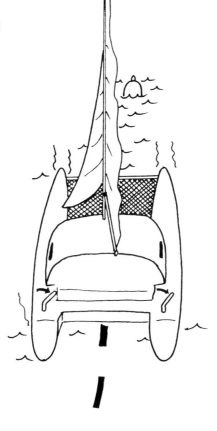

Sheeting the headsail on the opposite side to the desired tack will drive the multihull backwards and onto the tack required. When pointing in the desired direction tack the jib and sheet it in to sail away. Sail off on the jib first and once drive is established sheet in the mainsail. If you sheet in the mainsail first the multihull may stall and go into irons or drift onto the other tack.

APPARENT WIND

Apparent wind is the wind you can feel on a moving yacht. It is the combined effect of the true wind and the wind generated by the platform you are on moving. Multihulls generate a stronger apparent wind than monohulls due to the 'platform' moving faster. This can be both an advantage and a disadvantage.

The unwary can think that they are pointing high into the wind and going great speeds when in fact they are pointing well off the wind. In this situation a tack might be through 120 degrees or more. What happens is that the apparent wind is 'bent' with the accelerating boat speed as the multihull bears away from the true wind direction. If you are trying to point into the wind this is disastrous. To point high into the wind and generate the optimum speed toward a destination to windward you need to do some calculations and experimenting with your multihull. There will be an optimum windward speed for your size and shape of multihull. This will vary in given wind strengths and wave conditions and it is good seamanship to keep a notebook on the navigation table with useful data.

Multihull Seamanship Rule:
Understand and use apparent wind.

A typical data entry might be as follows:
Wind 15 knots. Seas slight. Full mainsail & working jib. Windward 9 knots, tacking angle 90 degrees.

There are a number of ways of determining the above figures. Computerised instruments will give a velocity made good (VMG) to windward. You also can calculate these figures if you know the boat speed and tacking angles.

Illustrated is an example of the effect on boat speed toward a windward point at different wind angles. The true wind is where the wind is coming from. The apparent wind is the 'wind you can feel' on the moving boat. The figures illustrated show the actual boat speed and the speed toward the windward point (VMG).

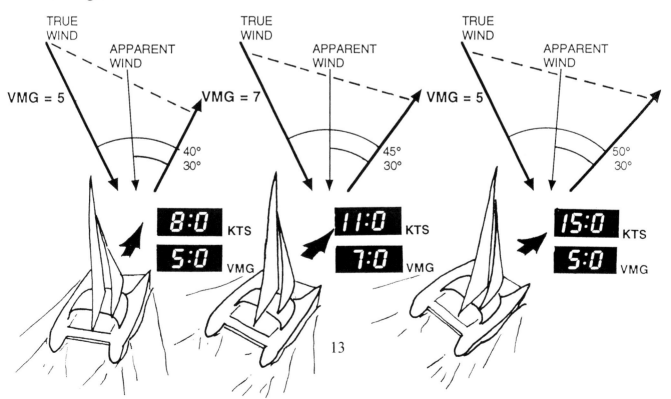

Sail shape

On day sailing catamarans, which are often over-canvassed, the lighter and faster the boat the flatter the sails need to be to allow for the increased apparent wind. In contrast offshore boats can all have efficient camber sails. Close sheeting is the answer to manage the apparent wind angle increase. The sheeting angle is the angle of the gap between the headsail and the mainsail. If the headsail is sheeted out wide then it is difficult to point high into the wind. In strong conditions this may make it impossible to sail effectively to windward.

In heavy conditions the true wind and apparent wind angles are much closer therefore fully reefed sails with shape are faster than flat feathering sails.

Storm jibs should have shape, not be flat blades. When your multihull has to beat off a lee shore in gale conditions this will be appreciated.

The weather and apparent wind

Cumulus clouds often mean there is vigorous mixing of the lower levels of the atmosphere and thus there is less difference in apparent wind angles between the waterline and the masthead. In these conditions less twist in the sail will maximise the use of apparent wind.

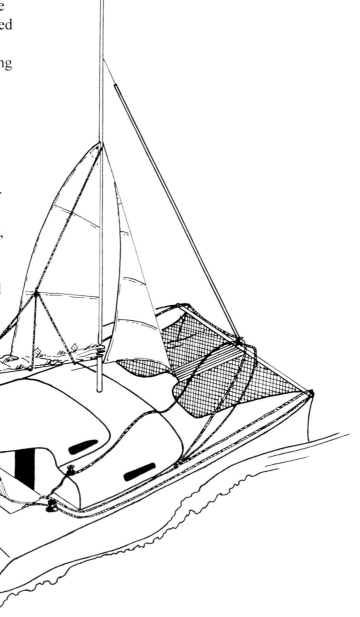

Racing use of apparent wind

Keep the sails centre of fullness about one third of the way back from the front, especially on the jib. The windward telltales should be just lifting. In most situations a high performance multihull will sail best downwind when the apparent wind is between 90 - 110 degrees apparent. Set your yacht up for this wind angle and bring the bows toward the wind until nearly luffing. As the yacht accelerates bear away keeping the power in the sails. If the sail collapses, let the yacht slow and start again. A modern performance multihull will carry the apparent wind direction, with sails set, to 110 -130 degrees apparent.

When racing downwind in this manner lift the centreboard until it is flush with the bottom. This reduces drag and maximises leeway.

On a catamaran which needs a centreboard for steering control then lift the leeward one flush and leave the windward one down a bit. By having only the windward centreboard slightly down when the windward hull lifts the catamaran will slip sideways and the boat will have less capsize potential.

Multihull Seamanship Rule:
Pull the centreboard(s) up when on all wind angles except sailing to windward.

BATTENS

Most multihulls have full length battens in the mainsail and on some occasions battened headsails.

The advantages of battens include longer sail life, reduced flogging when reefing, luffing or raising sails, elimination of furling (with lazyjacks), better sail shape and allowing a larger designed roach. Battens, especially round types, chafe on shrouds and increase sail wear unless chafe tabs are sewn onto the sail.

Battens exert a pressure on both ends of their pockets. Strong loads are taken by the end fittings. All too often the end fittings are bulky and have the potential to catch on reefing or lazyjack lines. You should ensure your system never catches. If dropping your mainsail results in the battens jamming the system up then change your batten system.

Multihull Seamanship Rule:
If you cannot reef with ease and speed then do not go to sea.

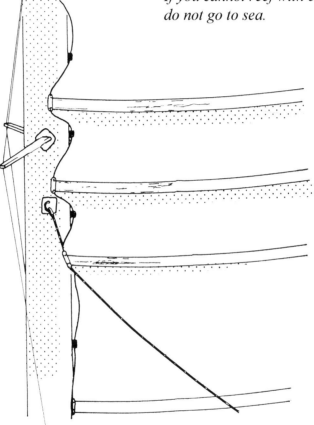

Seat belt webbing and leather are commonly used along the batten at shroud friction points as chafe protection. Protection is essential on the upper battens where wear is highest. All running backstays should be pulled forward off the sail when not in use. Failure to pull running rigging clear of rubbing on the mainsail will dramatically increase chafe.

A building gale is not the time to discover that your flogging mainsail batten end catches on a lazyjack. Batten entanglements can be avoided by either smoothing off the batten end (e.g. a material flap cover secured with velcro), setting the lazyjack lines differently, or terminating each batten at a slide or car.

Batten to mast attachments are vital to safety. If the luff is at all loose the batten will push forward and twist the fitting against the mast. There are stock fittings to reduce the batten to mast compression. These are like mini-goosenecks with the inboard end of the batten through bolted to ensure retention of the batten. An alternative is to have a way of tightening the luff from the mast head and the foot - a good halyard winch with two to one purchase on the mast head and a similar tackle arrangement or winch access to the cunningham eye (the downhaul point on the mainsail). The evenly tensioned luff will not allow the battens to ride forward.

When lowering the mainsail beware of the luff batten ends catching on the lazyjacks or spreader bars. When lowering the mainsail try and keep some downward pressure on the luff i.e. pull it down. This will stop the sail billowing forward and potentially catching on something. A well set up batten end/slide arrangement will allow you to release the main halyard with the sail dropping and furling neatly between the lazyjacks. If something can go wrong it usually will when you least want it to.

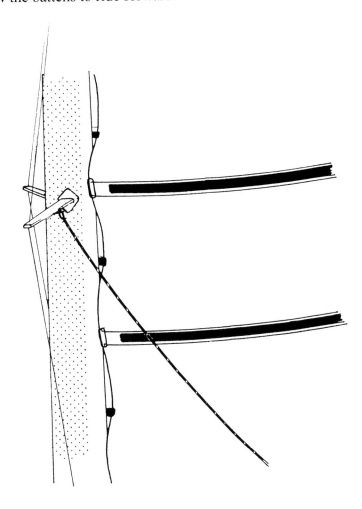

Simply moving the lazyjack take-off point from the mast to the spreader has solved this batten problem. The added chafe webbing will also stop the wear of the sail rubbing on the lazyjack lines.

Battens and gybing

Broken battens mean a torn sail unless they are removed quickly. Battens break during uncontrolled gybing, especially if a sidestay or running backstay is hit at speed. Round hollow battens (the lightest battens), need cross grain fibreglass wrapped around their ends to prevent crushing of the fibreglass.

Gybing should always be controlled. On full track multihulls this is easy because you can control the traveller throughout the gybe. On trimarans with only a central track then a barber hauler could be used. A barber hauler is a line from the boom to a point away from the central line of the yacht. Alternatively haul your mainsheet into the midline of the track and gybe around under jib and control the mainsail across on the track once gybed.

In heavy conditions it is best to keep boat speed up during the gybe to decrease the apparent wind on the sails. The gybe should be smooth but definite i.e. do not run square before gybing as this will increase the apparent wind.

The roach

The roach is the sail area of the mainsail aft of a line running from the clew to the head of the sail. The sail roach should not be too large. A big roach needs heavy battens to hold it out in moderate conditions. In light conditions these heavy battens do not readily allow an efficient aerofoil shape to be formed. It is in light conditions that you need the shape and the extra area to work. A mainsail with a large roach is predominantly a racing sail where the batten tension can be adjusted or different battens used for the conditions. If your multihull has a large roach and you use it for all sailing then have a system to allow a very deep reef in storm conditions (a fourth reef). Carry spare battens in case they break.

Reefing downwind

There is a trick to reefing the mainsail when sailing downwind. The problem to be overcome is to stop the battens from jamming and the sail from billowing out. Load the luff on the downhaul and then bear off onto a square run quickly. The apparent wind drops to zero for a few seconds. Release the mainsail halyard to the level required and the mainsail will slide quickly down.

BEAR AWAY!

BEACHING

Why beach your multihull?

Beaching is an easy (and cheap) way to do bottom cleaning, maintenance or emergency repairs. It can be done to escape rough weather or critical conditions. Multihulls suitable for beaching can be moored in shallow, high tidal areas. On occasions multihulls are beached by accident.

Bottom cleaning and maintenance

In the controlled situation there is one major rule.

Multihull Seamanship Rule:
When beaching know the bottom.

You will not park on a rock, reef or broken bottle if you check the area out first. This usually means via snorkel, view tube or in areas of poor visibility by feel.

When beaching there are a few minor rules that will help you avoid major problems.
• Avoid getting neaped. If you dry out at the top of the tide ensure that the following tides equal or making (getting higher). If the tides are falling (and you have bottomed at the 'neap' or highest) then you might be stuck. All it takes is a quick glance at the tide tables. If it is a neap tide wait until an hour or so after the high tide to dry out.
• Do not sit on the anchor. This occurs commonly in murky water or where there is a tide or no wind.
• Dry on a soft base. This equalises strains on the keel or hull bottom. Uneven rock or concrete need padding well to distribute the load.

20

• Watch the potential lee shore. An open beach or area susceptible to wind change can result in your multihull taking a severe pounding and possibly not being able to get off.

• Always lay a kedge into deep water as soon as possible after beaching. This may be the only way off if the wind changes.

Multihulls with fixed keels are less likely to have problems as a reduced area sits on the bottom. The keels are also fairly durable and designed to handle some impact. Unfortunately fixed keel multihulls require a greater tidal drop to get close to the beach. This is usually not a problem if you are in an area with reasonable tidal range.

21

Fixed underslung rudders should be capable of easily supporting the multihull at one end while the bow takes the weight at the other end. On a gently sloping beach this leaves most of the bottom accessible for working on. Multihulls with stern mounted rudders and no keels are the least suitable for beaching and cleaning and definitely need the bottom type carefully checked out.

If you are uncertain whether or not you can sit on your rudders assume you cannot. It is better to sail away not having completed your cleaning or maintenance than to discover you have bent your rudder shafts but managed to clean all the hulls.

Make sure the speed logs are not sat upon and that through hull fittings (e.g. water intakes) are patent and not clogged with mud when the hull is floating again.

Trimarans can have each float worked on by rotating the hulls around each tide if mooring parallel with the shoreline or by loading down one float when pointing up the beach. Ensure you check the area that the main hull will roll onto. Your boat is much heavier out of water and will not roll gently onto any obstruction.

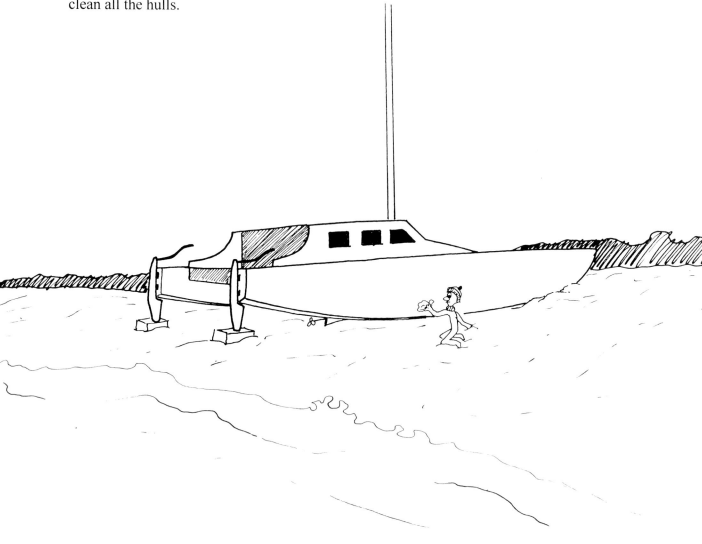

Beaching to escape rough weather

A multihull can ground and be winched or pulled up the beach in an emergency. This is a last ditch tactic but during the emergency is not the time to think it through for the first time. Now is.

As soon as the beach is touched the multihull is at risk of broaching in surf conditions. Lines need to be ready to run from each stern quarter and bow to stabilise the hulls.

Most deck winches will not pull a multihull up an incline. A tractor, truck or large on shore winch is usually needed.

Centreboards need to be up. Rudders should be swung up as the beach is touched. Fixed rudders can be dropped out but other steering is needed if a surf beach is to be passed through. Steering under outboard alone is not likely to work. The outboard will aerate or cavitate when the multihull starts surfing, losing steering when you most need it. Use a bridled drogue or a stern mounted sweep oar to control your direction.

Ensure the pull is as low as possible on the multihull to stop any ploughing effect. Unless special strong points are fitted then it might be useful to set up a harness around the hulls. The mast or deck winches are too high and should not be used to secure tow lines. Also check that the pull is straight. A bridle will assist this occurring. Any crabbing increases the drag. Rollers reduce friction but will indent into many hull materials. Sit the boat on a board or pieces of plywood and tow these up the beach.

BRIDLES

An easily set, adjustable, bridle system is a multihull sailors best friend. A bridle allows for the beam of the multihull to be utilised to create directional stability when anchored, towing a drogue or lying on a parachute sea anchor. It is also essential for a jury steering system.

Multihull Seamanship Rule:
Always have a bridle arrangement available.

How to set up a bridle

A bridle system needs the following characteristics:

• The rode (line to the anchor/drogue/parachute) should be adjustable in length and secured to a winch to enable it to be hauled in.

• The bridle arms should be at least the width of the beam. They also need to have enough length to be adjustable (especially when used to help steer the multihull). An exception to this rule is if you expect wind against tide conditions. Then the bridle arms should be short enough not to run under the centreboard(s).

• The bridle should be able to be set up on either the bows or the sterns.

There are many systems for securing the bridle arms to the rode. One of the best is using a rolling hitch. The two ends of the bridle arms should be spliced into one line and the line then tied to the rode with a rolling hitch.

A rolling hitch can be undone with load taken back on the rode and readily retied or slipped along for rode length adjustment. Throughout this manual are various bridle illustrations. Chose one that works for your multihull.

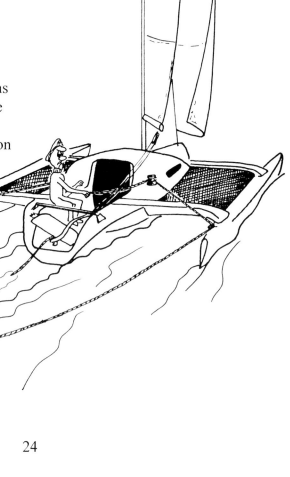

Bridle attachments

There are many ways of securing your bridle line to the anchor, drogue or parachute tether.

If your anchor line is chain then a simple strong locking clip attached to the ends of the bridle arms should work well. Many multihulls have their chain anchoring bridle permanently set up.

For attaching to rope a useful bridle knot, called a rolling hitch, is illustrated. This knot has a number of advantages. It can slide along the rope without having to be undone. It is able to be easily undone when the load is taken off the bridle arms and is on the tether line. It is also simple to learn.

Rolling hitch

The rolling hitch should be made with ropes of equal size. Splice the two ends of the bridle arms together so that only a single line needs to be tied to the tether. Practice the knot regularly and you will find lots of useful jobs for it (such as canopy tensioning, adjusting lazyjacks and tying down the dinghy).

CAPSIZE PREVENTION

Capsize is something every multihuller should be prepared for despite the fact that it is rare amongst cruising multihulls. It can happen and those crews and yachts prepared will survive to live and sail another day.

Capsize prevention is a broad topic and probably the main one relevant to multihull seamanship.

The three main areas included in this chapter are:
- Capsize prevention
    - The human factor
    - Wave factors
    - Wind factors
- Capsize preparation
    - Escape hatches
    - The inverted hull
    - Cockpit preparation
    - Cabin preparation
    - Calamity packs
- Post Capsize survival tactics
    - Immediate action
    - Inside the hull
    - Long term
    - Self rescue

The section on storm sailing should be included as part of the information on the sailing skills relevant to capsize prevention.

The human factor - avoiding the risk

All yachts are relatively safe in the shed at home or on the mooring but that is not what yachts are for. Capsize prevention begins with an attitude, some thinking and ends with preparation and practice.

The wind and wave conditions that can cause capsize can be predicated to a reasonable degree of accuracy. The pilot books, sailing directions and charts indicate wind and current averages, hurricane seasons, trade winds and areas of violent overfalls due to sub oceanic terrain. Treacherous gusts occur in coastal regions downwind from mountain ranges or sheer cliffs.

In your own area of sailing there is a wealth of local knowledge available. Technology can provide weather fax, regular sea state predictions and seasonal patterns. Other sailors can also help avoid disaster, particularly those who ply their trade on the water. All you have to do is ask.

The human factor is often last to be considered and the first to fail in extreme conditions. Sea-sickness, hypothermia, fear or simply the wrong attitude can all be factors in making the wrong decision at the wrong time. Many people are put at risk by having to sail to a time-table. Probably many lives lost also.

Many multihulls have been designed with certain sailing in mind. The human factors of finances, ego and ambition do not always parallel skill levels. It takes a brave person to step back from a project or cruise and say 'Can I do this with what I've got and what I know?'

Never-the-less multihulls are forgiving and a positive aspect of the human factor is that we rarely stop learning as we sail. Capsize is one end of the sailing spectrum that most will never experience but all should have given thought to.

Wave induced capsize

There are two aspects to wave induced capsize. These are sideways capsize due to the wave alone and tripping end-over-end (also known as pitch-poling). In many instances capsize will be a combination of the two. To understand the principles of capsize we will look at the two different types.

Beam on wave only capsize

A breaking wave may cause a yacht to capsize by rolling it around the central axis of the vessel.

Try not to get beam on to breaking waves. To reduce capsize risk distribute weight evenly away from the central axis - not into the bow or stern but out toward the sides. The term used to describe the effect of weight away from the central fore and aft axis is 'roll moment of inertia'. Simply put, a monohull, with centralised weight, has a low roll moment of inertia and is prone to wave capsize. Next comes a trimaran with predominantly centralised weight. The most resistant to wave capsize is a catamaran with the majority of the weight well away from the central axis. Bigger boats are harder to capsize because they have a greater roll moment of inertia.

WIND SWAMPED!

Other factors in beam on wave capsize include the tripping effect of keels and boards. Retracting centreboards enable the multihull to slide with the wave and further reduce the roll moment.

Multihull Seamanship Rule:
Wind way up, waves way up, centreboards way up.

If one centreboard on a catamaran needs to be down for steering then make it the windward one - any hull lifting will then allow the catamaran to slide sideways, reducing the capsize potential.

End on end wave capsize (pitch-poling)

Multihulls with fine bows have reduced stability in steep waves due to lack of buoyancy in the ends. Buoyant bows and weight centralised over the length of the yacht reduces the pitching and thus reduces the risk of the bows being driven under the water and the yacht tripping over a submerged hull.

If you already have a multihull with fine entry bows and low end buoyancy then the use of drogues and sea anchors needs to be well understood.

Older style trimarans with submersible floats are more susceptible to pitch-poling or broaching.

Pitch-poling is dramatically affected by the height of the centre of effort on the sails. Many racing multihulls that capsize do so while pressed hard sailing under spinnaker.

After surfing down a wave a multihull may slow in the trough or at the slope of the face of the wave ahead. The apparent wind then increases as the vessel stalls. Overpowered and stalled there is no way to go but over. The chapter on Storm Sailing discusses tactics to use downwind.

29

Sheet systems

Wind induced capsize is bad seamanship and is preventable. All sheet systems can tangle and snag.

Multihull Seamanship Rule:
Always carry a knife suitable for cutting sheets quickly.

Every cockpit should have a knife ready in a sheath strapped near the sheet lines. Kevlar and Spectra braid needs a knife with a 'sawing teeth' section. Alternatively use a hacksaw.

Most modern multihulls use winches to help sheeting in or hauling up sails. On shorthanded yachts self-tailing winches are the norm. The quickest manual way of releasing sheets is to flick them free from a 'cam' cleat - not to have them permanently in the self-tailing part of the winch.

Remember that 'jamb' cleats are different from 'cam' cleats and can be impossible to release under load. For the sheet to run freely it should have the minimum number of turns on the winch that holds the load. Leave the mainsheet with only one or two turns around the winch before inserting it in a cam cleat.

Multihull Seamanship Rule:
Never leave a rope in a self tailing jammer.

Self tailing jammers take longer to release and need the rope to be turned around the winch to be released.

Over-rides lock sheets and are disastrous in an emergency. If an over-ride occurs, immediately work to release it. Once the over-ride is free work out why it occurred and solve the problem. Often one winch always over-rides; usually due to the angle the sheet approaches the winch.

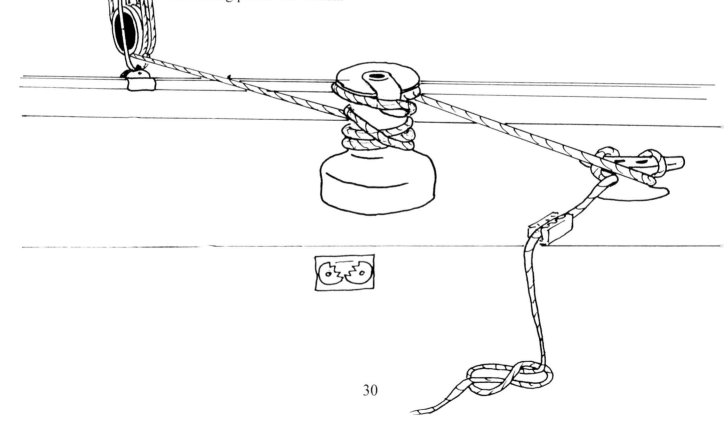

On multihulls that use purchase systems (multiple sheave blocks) rather than winches the sheets should still finish in a cam cleat. The purchase systems are usually mainsheet systems and they require a longer length of line (and thus time) to run free to release the boom. Rapid release of the mainsheet is essential so devise a system that has a quick release component accessible in an emergency.

Multihull Seamanship Rule:
The loose end of loaded sheets should always run freely.

Automatic sheet release systems

These use two principles - mainsheet load or heel angle.

Non-electronic systems all have drawbacks and are rarely seen. When using the principle of a pendulum they work by reaching a certain degree at which the sheet is released. This is effective but is very prone to letting go in a rough seaway due to the bouncing around of wave action.

Mainsheet load systems need to be finely set by trial and error and again are prior to inappropriate release due to shock loads. Both manual techniques need a winch free line. If a purchase system is used then the line will have to be long and thus more readily snagged and slower to release. Electronic systems have yet to be perfected. Ideally these would operate on a hydraulic mainsheet system with the ability to dump the load immediately given the right data input about heel angle, speed and mainsail load.

Reefing systems

Multihull Seamanship Rule:
If you think you need to reef then reef.

It is better to be under-powered and upright than over-powered and inverted.

When sailing downwind reef the mainsail before the headsails and reef early. An overpowered main will drive the bows under whereas a reefed main can be depowered easily. Be aware of the low apparent wind but a high true wind when sailing downwind. The true wind may cause capsize if you stall while surfing.

When sailing upwind and reaching then reef to keep the yacht in balance (or with slight weather helm). This will aid manoeuvrability and if steering is lost the yacht will not drive away under a gust.

A well shaped and reefed mainsail will make your multihull go faster than a flat, inefficient, feathering mainsail. Storm jibs also should have a good shape. Tight sheeting angles should be used to work the high apparent wind at speed.

Monohulls reef to the average wind speed and lean over or flog sails in gusts. Multihulls need to reef to the gust speed.

Multihull Seamanship Rule:
Reef to the gust wind speed.

There is a useful trick to reefing when sailing downwind. The preparation required is to have the minimum number of mainsail slides necessary (these are what jam) and to have the ability to winch the luff down. The trick is to load the luff downhaul and then quickly bear away to reduce the apparent wind.

31

CAPSIZE PREPARATION

After capsize and making your way to the top of the inverted multihull you need immediate access to the following:
- Lifejacket
- Liferaft
- Calamity pack
- Escape hatch (or tools to make one)
- Knife

If you cannot get these things when capsized then redesign your multihull before it occurs! This section looks at the ways to maximise survival chances by being prepared.

Capsize hatches

These need to be above the inverted waterline. If your particular design of multihull has capsized then contact the survivors and find out at what level the hulls floated. An access hatch too close to the water can create problems of ease of entry or exit and having to get wet all the time. The hatch does not have to be in the perfect spot if you have the ability to make another one.

Multihull Seamanship Rule:
Always have the ability to access the hulls when inverted.

Ideally the access hatch would be along the keel line - but this is not structurally possible. Your multihull designer should be able to give information about positioning a hatch.

Multihulls made of material that cannot be readily penetrated (e.g. aluminium or kevlar) must have an access hatch. The minimum diameter of an access hatch should be 450 mm and be able to be opened from either inside or outside. If a hatch cannot be readily positioned then there are a number of options.

Capsize hatch options

1. A small porthole that can be opened when inverted and the tools reached to cut an access hatch. Have suitable areas marked on the hulls so that you are not cutting into bulkhead areas or tanks.

2. A hatchet or ice pick strapped to the netting or back of a beam. This can be used to cut at a predetermined site.

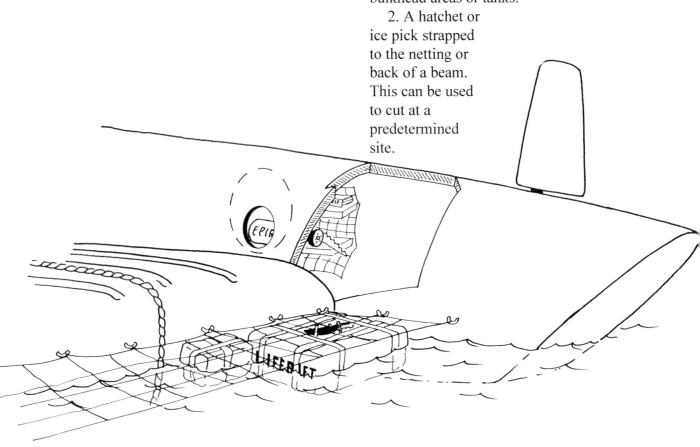

Kevlar is very difficult to cut with an axe. A hole should be made with a pick (e.g. ice pick) and then a cutting blade inserted to make the hole. Save the piece cut out as a simple hinge can be made to make a hatch cover to exclude the elements.

The inverted hull

The bottom colour should be visible. Rescue Orange is the recommended colour. Antifouling colours such as white or blue do little to facilitate rescue.

All inverted walking areas (trimarans wing decks and catamarans bridgedecks) should have suitable hand holds, footholds and non-skid areas. At least two stout ropes should be set beneath the wing structures, one close to each side of the multihull and bent (not spliced) into a secure anchorage at each end of the wing structure.

If your hulls are not capable of providing live-in inverted accommodation then there should be adequate rope attachments to 'spider' your liferaft between hulls. The ties to the liferaft need to be strong and chafe resistant. Regular checking of these attachments are needed to ensure you do not lose the mother-ship.

Standard liferafts do not have adequate tethering points. Request additional, reinforced attachment tags to be added to your liferaft during its next service.

Automatic inflation devices are not required on a multihull liferaft. After a capsize it could auto-inflate under the trampoline.

The liferaft is your chance at last ditch survival. The supplies most off-shore liferafts are packed with are appropriate and should not be reduced. Consider adding an EPIRB (emergency positioning indicating radio beacon) to your liferaft when packed. Capsize is but one disaster. Your multihull may be run down by a ship, hit a whale or burn - with nothing left but the liferaft.

Cockpit preparation for capsize

Multihull Seamanship Rule:
A tie for everything and everything tied.

The cockpit hatch boards should be capable of being secured from both inside and out. The boards should be tied and accessible even if they are floating underwater. Cockpit lockers usually hold important survival tools - fishing lines, boathooks etc. Ensure the lockers have secure clasps. Portable fuel tanks should be tied on.

Calamity packs

Calamity packs have added advantages on multihulls. Set these waterproof packs up to contain essential equipment for survival when inverted. Standard equipment should include flares, distress V sheet, signalling mirror, torch and knife. Of relevance to survival inverted you could add the following:
• portable radar reflector (empty aluminium wine bladders do not work).
• fishing line and hooks.
• a file and hacksaw blades/hacksaw or keyhole saw (to make a hatch or jury rig a mast).
• flippers, mask and snorkel.
• hand held radio in a properly designed waterproof bag (strongly recommended).
• hand operated desalinator.
• hand drill and bits for starting hacksaw cuts in fibreglass, kevlar or carbon composite hulls.

Sails, either in sailbags or loose on the floor of the cockpit or cabin are a major hazard after capsize.

Multihull Seamanship Rule:
Close sailbags firmly and secure the bag to the hull.

Capsize cabin preparation

Lie on the floor and look at the roof. Imagine everything upside down and make a mental list of where things would be. If possible create an area inside one of the hulls that will remain dry in the inverted position. Ask your multihull designer where the inverted waterline should be. There are many simple ways of securing objects so they will be available to use and not washed out the hatches.

Have tags sewn into the corner of mattresses and tie them to the bunks. If the ties have enough line on them the mattresses can become hammocks upside down and may provide a valuable area above the inverted waterline.

Stowage netting should have strong elastic closures so that when it is tossed about the contents do not fall out. Unsecured carpet is a major hazard as it creates a blanket over the entire cabin contents - including any persons.

Lockers must have secure clasps. Essential tools (all of them!) should be bagged and the bag secured to the hull. Keep clothing in bags in lockers. A simple tether from the bag to a tie-down fitting may save someone from developing hypothermia or exposure problems.

Batteries must be secure and not leak when inverted. Ideally, store batteries so that the terminals are above the inverted waterline. Batteries need to be quickly isolated to prevent power drainage.

If batteries are enclosed, and the terminals greased or sprayed with water retardant, very little or no chlorine gas will be produced. The batteries may be salvaged and used to power lighting or radios. Store batteries separately from the accommodation area.

Lighting systems can be positioned to provide light upside down. A simple inversion switch on a torch will provide essential light to orientate yourself in the event of night time capsize.

Water storage must be secured and have easily accessed closing valves. The loss of water when inverted is disastrous to long term survival. Some tanks are designed not to drain when tipped upside down.

Multihull Seamanship Rule:
Always carry a spare water container that is totally separate, sealed and secured to the hull.

Emergency equipment

All freshwater containers should have an air gap so that they will float.

All through-hull fittings should have seacocks and wooden plugs to ensure they can always be closed. Hatches should be able to be opened from both inside and outside the hull.

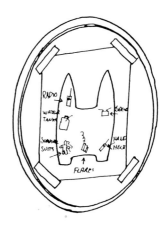

A map of the hull layout and where vital objects are stored may save valuable searching time for unfamiliar crew members. It also would stop unnecessary swimming or hull penetrating. Draw the map in waterproof ink on the inside of the escape hatch. A waterproof plastic map could similarly be stored in the calamity pack.

The options for storing the EPIRB (Emergency Position Indicating Radio Beacon) include:
- at the companionway entrance
- inside the escape hatch
- lashed to, or inside, the liferaft
- in the calamity pack (the best position).

No matter where the EPIRB is positioned it must be available without great effort. An EPIRB will not send a signal through a carbon fibre hull. Place it outside.

Survival suits are one-piece hooded suits that are insulated. They greatly aid in survival in situations where hypothermia is a real risk. A multihull sailor who ventures into colder latitudes would be well advised to invest in a set. At the very minimum a space blanket for hypothermia management should be carried.

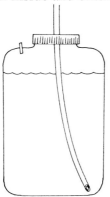

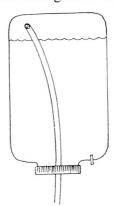

CAPSIZE SURVIVAL TACTICS

Imminent capsize

If you are in borderline conditions and capsize is about to happen then the best place to be is in the hull and well padded from sharp edges and objects. If you have to be on the helm then think through what you will do if capsize occurs. Once under water it may be difficult to undo the harness.

Multihull Seamanship Rule:
Always wear a safety harness that can be released under load.

A hook type attachment would be suitable for the other end.

When the multihull is inverted there may be air traps in the cockpit but none are certain. Unfortunately going without a safety harness in such conditions puts you at risk of being swept overboard. The cockpit design and layout will determine the best option.

Multihull Seamanship Rule:
Test your harness safety systems.

On a warm day jump into the water in your wet weather jacket and see if the harness lines run free. Get someone to put load on the line and see if you can undo the snap shackle at your end.

Post capsize - immediate action

If you are outside and on the inverted hull secure yourself. Tie a line to any strong point. Determine where everyone is and their condition. Immediate priority is anyone else outside who is not on the inverted hulls. Do not leave the vessel in an attempt to rescue anyone without being securely attached to the hull by a line strong enough to support both of you. Do not swim under the multihull unless absolutely essential. There will be a mass of lines, debris, sails and wire floating around the cockpit area.

Knocking on the hull will determine if anyone is inside and alert. The prevailing conditions will determine how rapidly the hull should be accessed. Cold, wild conditions accelerate the onset of hypothermia. Open or create an escape hatch. Check the crew inside and then start securing everything. Do not let anything drift away if possible.

Multihull Seamanship Rule:
When capsized secure everything as soon as possible.

The main hatch will usually be underwater. Surge through this will cause many items to be lost. Close the hatch. The escape hatch also may be partially closed to increase cabin temperature - but do not close it completely. Ear pain occurs with the rapid changes in cabin pressure due to surging water and crewman have died from lack of fresh available air.

Isolate the batteries. Close water tanks and any fuel lines.

When everything is stabilised and it is safe to venture out, then there are a few jobs to do to ensure the structural integrity of the inverted multihull. If the mainsail is still sheeted then try and release or cut the sheet line. The loads created by the mainsail are enough to cause significant structural damage.

Inside the hull on capsize

If possible secure the main hatch to stop every loose object from washing out. If everyone is inside the hull there is no urgency to open the escape hatch as long as there is a supply of fresh air. Possible sources are the log, water drainage holes, toilet systems, depth sounder ports etc.

Secure any free sheets or lines. Often the anchor is hanging free - securing it may enable it to be used later to stop the capsized multihull from drifting onto reefs or through the surf.

Long term capsize survival

You can aid your chances of rescue by assisting the searchers. If someone is to find you it will usually be via radar, electronic direction indicators or radio. Discovery via direct vision is unlikely without the aid of flares or radar reflectors mounted on some sort of jury mast. Make an assessment of the likelihood of available assistance and prepare accordingly. A jury rigged mast using either spinnaker pole, boom or oars can be rigged on the upturned hull. To this you can hoist metal radar reflecting objects (ideally a portable radar reflector from the calamity pack). Coloured material can be flown for direct vision. Your multihull will lie low in the water. The higher you can put anything the greater chance of being sighted.

Power for lighting and radio is possible if the batteries are salvaged quickly. Even a solar panel will survive immersion if it is dried and corrosion sprayed after salvage. In your tool box have a can of water corrosion treatment. Remove any electronics from underwater as soon as possible and spray them.

If you have radio power then conserve batteries by only transmitting when there is likelihood of someone hearing. Stick to the distress times - on the hour until 3 minutes past and on the half hour until 33 minutes past. Your radio can be used as a directional bearing for helicopters, ships and planes fitted with radio direction finders. Cellular telephones are not a substitute for a marine radio as they are not able to be tracked.

An EPIRB will usually facilitate quick rescue - more so if it is a satellite type. Any multihull going offshore should have the satellite compatible EPIRB.

EPIRB's are not infallible and the batteries do run out but they are your immediate close link with the rescue organisations. Ensure the tether is secure and the antennae fully extended. EPIRB's are designed to be deployed in the water outside the cabin. Flares, signalling mirror and distress V flag should be on hand for rapid use. Secure them near the hatch so the person on watch has immediate access. An overhead aircraft can fly from horizon to horizon in under a minute.

Self rescue

Multihull Seamanship Rule:
Think carefully before leaving your capsized multihull.

It may be tempting to set sail in the dinghy for a distant shore. The chance of surviving in a dinghy for any length of time is much less than the chances aboard your yacht. Dinghies sail poorly and unless wind, currents and expected weather are very predictable then the risks are high.

Remember that most capsized multihulls are righted and sail again, often with only a minimum of cost. If you abandon your yacht you give up some rights to it. Try and arrange a recovery operation before abandoning the vessel.

Self preservation

Exposure protection should be started from the outset.

In a crisis, under maritime law, the skipper remains skipper. In reality the most enthusiastic and confident person takes control. All decisions need discussion. Never expect other survivors to be aware of your thoughts. Communicate.

The 'on watch' person should be sheltered from prevailing wind and spray. Use sun protection at all times. If it is cold then put as much clothing on as possible. In cold conditions a thick layer of wet clothing is warmer than a thin layer of dry. Huddle together to maintain warmth. By wringing wet clothing out it is possible to dry internal layers with body warmth alone.

Sea ulcers can develop from pressure points and small lacerations if the following is not observed. Move about when lying around. Exercise regularly. Pad your bed position. Treat every cut as serious. Clean and wash the area with fresh water. Dress any wound and use antibacterial ointments as available. Psyche needs careful management. The status of skipper and crew often alters as each confronts his or her own fears.

Multihull Seamanship Rule:
In a crisis communicate.

Shared fears, thoughts and ideas promote survival.

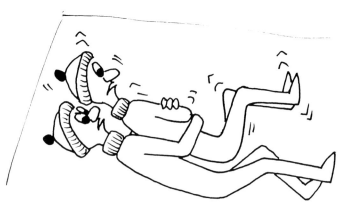

CARGO

As a rough rule of thumb a multihull can carry 1/3 of its weight in 'cargo' with ease. By loading the yacht to half of its weight the vessel is straining. Ask the designer for the designed loaded weight and do not exceed this as to do so will overload the structure and may lead to failure. When reading literature about different designs there are lots of confusing terms. Examples include 'designed displacement', 'displacement', 'weight' and 'payload'. None of these figures may tell you what you need to know. The displacement is the weight of water the vessel will displace when floating. The 'designed displacement' is the weight of water displaced at the drawn water line. The 'weight' may or may not include sailing essentials such as all sails, anchors, safety equipment, fixtures and fittings. The 'payload' ability similarly might exclude many essential items and the true ability to carry extra goods (like guests and their baggage, food and toys) may be dramatically reduced after accounting for them. What you need to know is what is the boat weight ready for sea and what is its ability to carry extra non essential weight.

The distribution should be designed to reduce pitching - as low and as central along the fore and aft axis as possible. This is easily designed in a trimaran with floor based water tanks and storage. In the catamaran the cargo weight should be equally divided between hulls. Be careful not to be balanced at the start of a voyage and grossly unbalanced at the end when the water tanks or fuel tanks are much lower.

Multihull Seamanship Rule:
Never overload a multihull and go to sea.

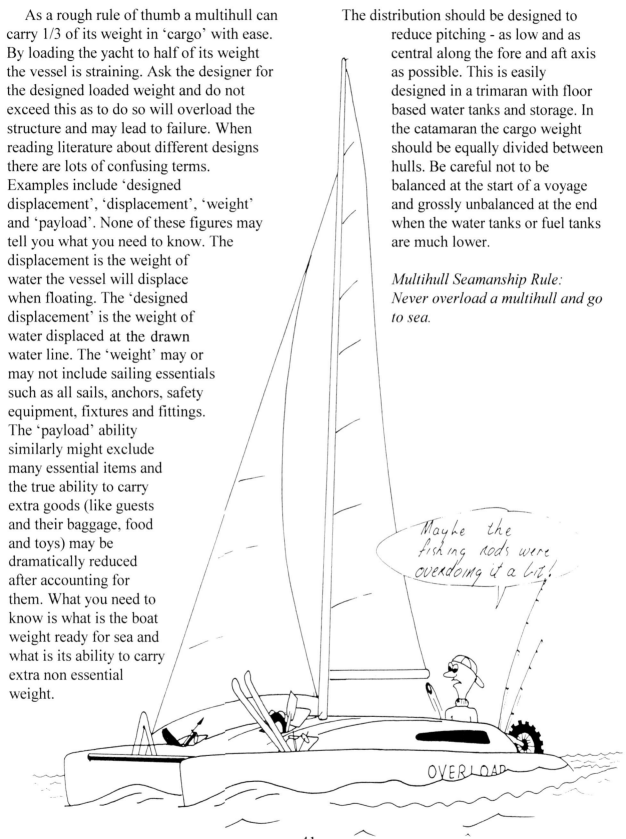

CENTREBOARDS

Centreboards give increased performance to windward over fixed skegs and provide greater 'beachability' due to reduced draft with the boards up. The two types of centreboards are daggerboards (boards which slide down in a slot like a dagger) and pivoting boards which pivot back into a long slot. Pivoting boards are not as popular as daggerboards due to the increased turbulence of the exposed long slot and the fact that the centre of lateral resistance moves aft when the pivoting board is partially raised.

To maximise the sailing advantages use them in the following ways:

Windward centreboard use

When sailing to windward in light wind to moderate winds have the centreboard(s) fully down. In very light winds have only one centreboard down on a catamaran to reduce the wetted surface area (and thus friction).

To windward in heavy wind partially retract the board(s) to reduce the pressures on the case and board(s).

Downwind centreboard use

On a catamaran the boards should be adjusted to balance the helm. When broad reaching this usually means the windward board half down and the leeward centreboard should be nearly fully up. When running have both centreboards nearly fully up. A small amount of board down will improve downwind steering. At high boat speed the turbulence from the centreboard may affect the rudders so retract them fully.

On trimarans the centreboard is usually pulled up completely to reduce drag and turbulence and to enable the multihull to point

slightly higher (and thus have a higher apparent wind) while slipping sideways to create optimum speed downwind.

When sailing in shallow waters on multihulls without kick up rudders it is a good idea to keep the centreboards down to a depth slightly beyond that of the rudders. It is usually easier to get off following a grounding when it involves the centreboard(s). Damage to a centreboard bottom is preferable to that of the rudder(s).

Centreboard and case design

A sacrificial section on the base of the board(s) will save having to rebuild a complete board. To manufacture such a board make one of normal size and then cut off the lower 20-40 cm and then glue it back on.

The centreboard case should be a lot stronger than the board. If you run aground it is cheaper to build a board than repair a broken case.

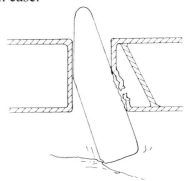

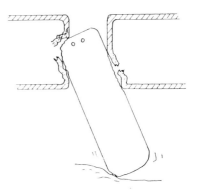

42

If the centreboard and case are angled forward the board may be driven up on impact and avoid case damage. Unfortunately this design catches all floating weed and net.

Some centreboards pivot back into the hull. If the control lines are weak enough to break on running aground then this also saves damage. The problem with this design is the long slot required and the associated turbulence and drag associated with water travelling over the open slot. Rubber covers help but do not solve this dilemma.

Centreboard cases can be built with sacrificial pads to absorb the impact. Alternatively, you can build a box section behind the case to enclose any rupture so the hull integrity is not voided.

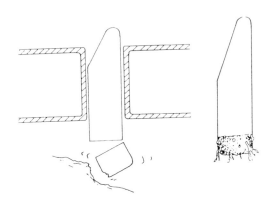

Some centreboards drop low in their box to save weight. This has the unfortunate result of distributing any impact over a small area of the case - increasing the likelihood of case rupture and major damage.

Centreboard controls

Most centreboards are impossible to raise or lower when the multihull is under way. This is because the very function of the centreboard is to increase lateral resistance and transmit this effect to the hull and rig. This force jams the board against the side of the case. To raise or lower centreboards you have to break the lateral resistance. This can be done by rounding up and losing way, by bearing away and slowing down or by ooching - swinging the rudder from side to side and making the hulls zig-zag rapidly. On the race course the time to raise and lower cerntreboards is during tacking or gybing or, best of all, after rapidly bearing away and removing the lateral load on the board. Most centreboard control lines are fed back to the cockpit. Have a winch available to assist in loading up the line so that when the tack is under way the board will pop up (or down) as the lateral resistance is taken off.

Centreboard hints

To service your centreboard it is easy to raise it out of the case by using a halyard.

Antifoul any section of the centreboard that remains in the water. Ensure that this section does not jam in the case.

Keels

The advantages of keels are low maintenance and no cabin obstruction. Keels also provide protection for motor propellers and are a solid base with which to beach on. The disadvantages are reduced windward performance, slower tacking, an increased pitching due to increased central buoyancy, an inability to retract the keel when sideways drift is needed (e.g. storm survival - see Cyclone chapter) and reduced beach access due to increased draft and need for a greater tidal range to 'dry out' on a beach.

CHILDREN

A multihull that is safe for children requires an understanding of the unique features and potential problems inherent in a yacht that uses beam for stability. Multihulls heel less which makes a 'home at sea' much more comfortable and stable. Multihulls also accelerate faster and may catch the unwary or child without support. Trampolines, open deck areas and loaded sheet ropes all create an environment that needs thought in layout and education for children.

There are three areas that will be addressed:
• Cabin design features
• Deck design safety
• Safety hints.

Cabin design and children

On catamarans hand rails need to be provided to allow young children to safely access the bridgedeck from the hulls. On full bridgedeck cabin catamarans the bunks are often at bridgedeck level and there is a big drop to the floor level in the hull. Ensure the bunks have a rail to stop them from falling out and the ladder to the bunk has good hand rails. Children will still fall - it's part of the learning process - so remove objects in likely drop zones!

The corners of navigation tables, stoves, bulkheads and general furniture should be rounded or padded. A floor with good non slip and cushioning will help keep children on their feet without too many bruises. As an experiment crawl around your boat on your knees to get a feel of the danger areas when you are only a metre tall.

Consider where you would put the children in ultimate weather conditions and imminent capsize. Ideas could include bunking them on the hull floor near the escape hatch with the roof and walls padded with attached cushions (have the tie down points prepared before you depart. A small chore but reassuring). Another suggestion used was strapping them in a car seat again attached to the hull side near the escape hatch. Babies in basinets can be gimballed in a net bag secured strongly to the hull. All these areas need to be above the capsized waterline and away from potential flying debris.

On deck

Although multihulls are stable they tend to move quicker to wind and wave action. For this reason children need the added safety of toerails, flat deck area, sturdy stanchions and netting. As a general rule children should not be out of the cockpit unless supervised. Consider a running lifeline so that the child is always tethered to the boat. The line should be long enough to allow mobility but short enough not to allow them to reach the water should they go over the side.

Grab rails for walking around the deck need to be at a height that they can reach. This is particularly important near sloped deck areas.

Access onto multihulls is sometimes difficult with high chine vessels. Stanchion rail gates need locks that children cannot easily undo. For boarding high freeboard multihulls consider stern steps or a sugar scoop stern with a boarding ladder.

Ask yourself if one of the children falls overboard can they climb aboard themselves? If not, can you climb aboard with them in your arms?

Children love climbing in and out of hatches and on multihulls they are usually over bunk areas. Ensure the hatches have positive locking and are secure in both the open and closed positions.

Trampoline netting can vary enormously in weave size. Open weave nets which allow a small arm or foot through are a potential source of sprains and strains.

Children need to feel that they are useful. An adjustable helm seat which allows them to see forward and learn to steer is popular.

Safety hints

Lifejackets need to be lifejackets - not buoyancy vests. They also need to be of an appropriate size for the child. Consider where these are stored. If you have an arrangement for securing the child in storm conditions ensure they can be secured with their lifejacket on.

Children with any special health problems or needs should be catered for in the calamity pack. For example, babies might need a spare bottle and teat in liferaft.

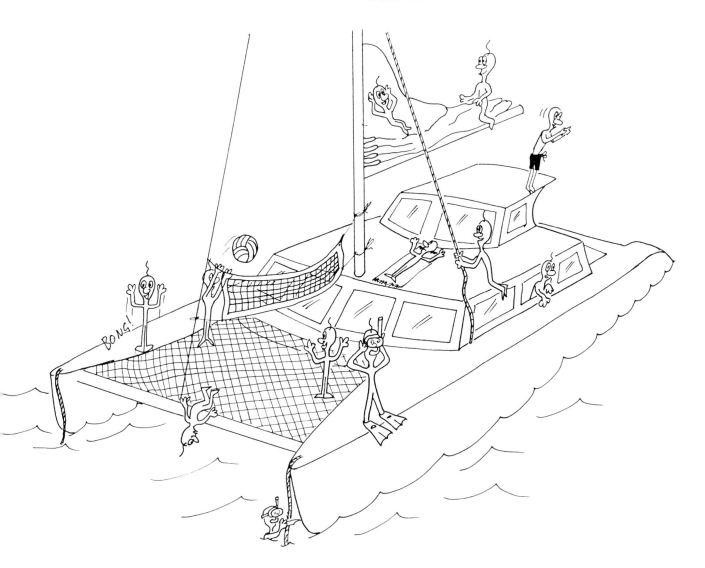

COLLISION

Bilge pumps

Multihulls by definition have multiple compartments, some interconnected, some independent. The bilges are often so shallow that pumps cannot be permanently fitted.

Multihull Seamanship Rule:
A high capacity portable bilge pump is a must for a multihull.

Each bilge pump should have two long, permanently attached hoses. Lanyards need to be ready for securing the pump on deck.

Watertight bulkheads

Each bow and both sterns should have watertight bulkheads. This is not to say that the areas cannot be used for other purposes - as long as the access ports are watertight and strong enough to withstand flooded water pressure. Many watertight compartments have inspection ports. Design a hose fitting (inserted through an inspection port) that will enable each compartment to be pumped out without a crew member having to hold the hose. Hoses should be long enough to enable pumping of all major compartments from the safety of the cockpit or similar location.

Securing the damage

Most multihulls will flood but not sink when the hull(s) are penetrated. The exception is aluminium multihulls.

Surging internal water creates high stress loads on all hull types. Seal the hole as soon as possible and pump the water clear. Sail to minimise loads and reduce hull stresses. A flooded hull will force the multihull to 'drag' off centre. Sailing may be impossible. Remember the availability of your sea anchor to help the hulls settle into a suitable angle to effect repairs.

Carry the equipment to effect repairs. This might include a portable or hand held drill, self tapping screws, sheets of plywood, silicone sealer and rapid drying underwater epoxy.

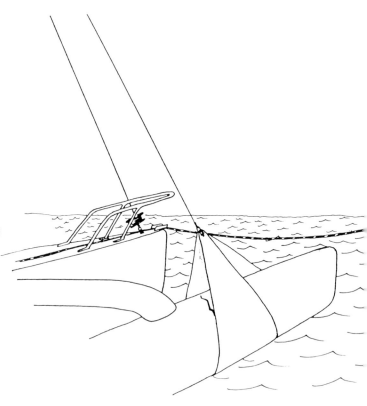

CREW & PASSENGERS

Every time a person steps aboard your multihull for a sail it is good seamanship to go through a safety check. The more challenging the sail the more comprehensive the information although there are a few basics that should be covered every time. Make sure any monohull sailors listen as the safety characteristics of multihulls differ.

The routine information should include:

- lifejacket storage and use
- lifebuoy and danbuoy release
- man overboard drill
- radio operation
- how to start the motor
- how to lower sails.

It is a good idea to have someone in the crew to act as backup in case the skipper is the one that goes overboard or is sick.

Warn everyone about the ability for multihulls to accelerate quickly and respond rapidly to helm changes.

Multihull Seamanship Rule:
Keep one hand for the boat. Hold on.

Explain that the sheet ropes are highly loaded and that nobody should stand over, sit on or hold them. Similarly the winches are a danger point because the ropes are in quick release catches and can occasionally be knocked free.

The mast base on rotating rigs is not the place to admire the view. The rotating spanner can shear ankles off. Everybody should be aware of this and if they do need to be in the area then show how the rotation spanner is secured.

If embarking on an ocean voyage then the crew needs a full run down on the other safety features. Those specific to multihulls are included throughout this book. Keep a copy on board and have it read.

A good seamanship idea is to have a checklist of the information to be explained stored near the starter key or helm.

CYCLONES

Lightweight, racing multihulls have survived cyclones intact and upright. A multihull needs special management to survive. It needs to be worked, not left to the whim of the conditions.

Multihull Seamanship Rule:
Know where cyclones are, where you are and where you are both going.

Cyclones have roughly predictable tracks. This information is available in pilot books, ocean manuals and from most radio bases. Use everything possible to get an accurate assessment of where the cyclone is heading. Know accurately where you are in relation to the approaching cyclone.

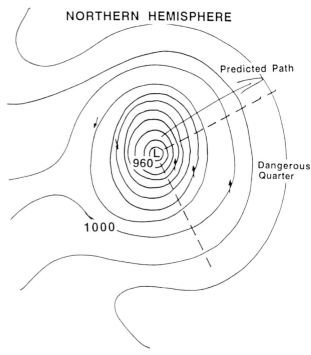

NORTHERN HEMISPHERE

Predicted Path

Dangerous Quarter

960

1000

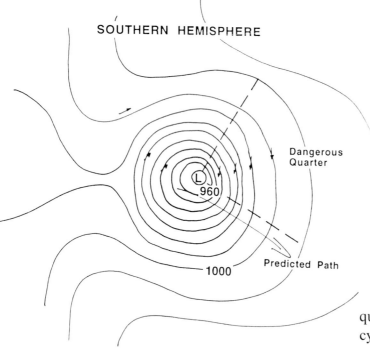

SOUTHERN HEMISPHERE

Dangerous Quarter

960

1000

Predicted Path

In the Southern Hemisphere the place not to be is ahead and to the left of the cyclone. This is the 'dangerous quadrant'. Running downwind from here will suck you into the worst conditions.

In the Northern Hemisphere the dangerous quadrant it ahead and to the right of the cyclone centre.

Multihull Seamanship Rule:
Always draw a diagram of your cyclone predictions.

It helps to get a confident understanding of where to go.

48

Cyclones and mooring

There are occasions when nothing can be saved. Never-the-less you can maximise the chance of your multihull surviving a cyclone on the mooring by utilising some of the following hints.

Moor in the most protected area as far inland as possible. Mangrove swamps are a popular option in shallow water with lines spidered in every direction. To get into these raise centreboards and rudders. Be aware that cyclones always bring exceptionally high tides due to the low atmospheric pressure. Watch for mooring lines tearing free and flooding of areas that might compromise the safety of your multihull.

At sea in a cyclone

Survival tactics are covered in the chapter on Storm Sailing. More than anything else it is important to prepare and initiate your plans early. It is virtually impossible to set and release a parachute sea anchor once you are in 60 knots of wind and ten metre waves.

It is possible to continue to sail and crawl off a lee shore under mast and storm rig given knowledge of you multihulls drift characteristics and balance with rudders, centreboard(s) and rig. The time not to learn is during the cyclone!

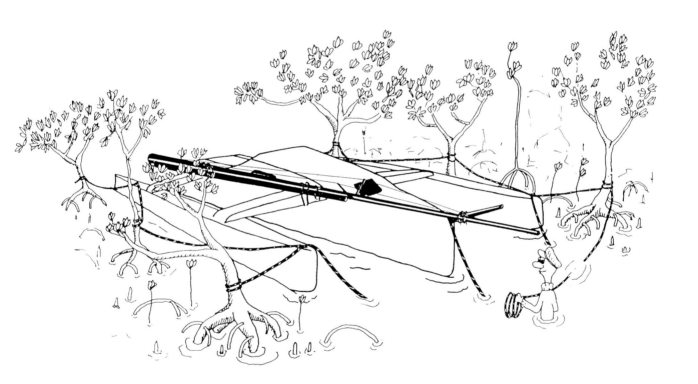

Reduce windage to a minimum. Remove all sails, stow the boom, remove all deck lines and netting. If possible lower the mast or remove it.

Increase the ballast low in the yacht. One way of doing this is to fill the water tanks (a good idea as water may not be available after the cyclone has destroyed land piping and supply).

A lot of damage is done by flying debris and other boats on the move. If possible get away from them.

It is not advisable to stay aboard during a cyclone. Get onto the land and leave your multihull to fend alone.

If the multihull is in an area of wave action then flooding is probably not a good idea. The internal surge will load lines and bulkheads. In very protected areas flooding may help.

On a swing mooring triple the lines - including the bridle. Ensure the mooring block is adequate, the attachments strong and the lines chafe protected.

Any breakdown in your mooring or problems from other boats are unlikely to be helped by a crew present aboard. All you would be doing is risking your life. Imagine trying to tie a line or work while standing on the roof of your car travelling 150 kilometres per hour.

If you have to anchor then do so with as much thought as possible. Pick a protected area, shallow and with a good holding bottom. Run as much chain out as you have.

It is very important to check your neighbours. The one boat that is unattended will be the one to break free and wreak havoc.

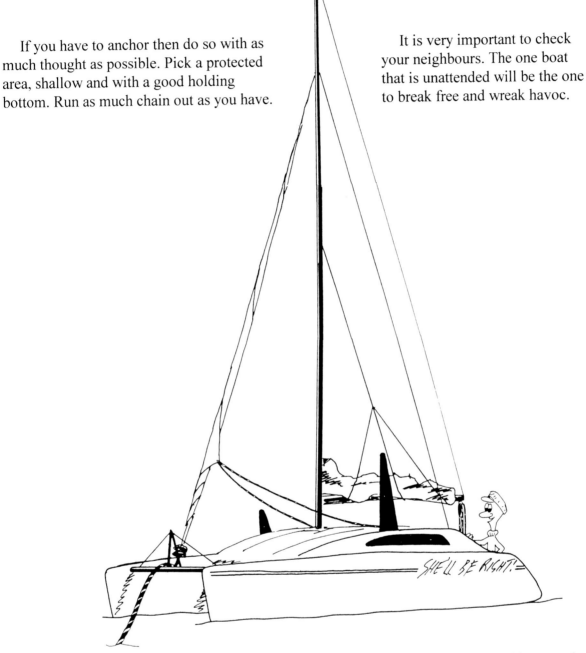

SHE'LL BE RIGHT!

Any lines need lots of chafe protection and always bridle the multihull. To reduce the chance of windage flipping your multihull it is suggested that buckets, bags or even a parachute hanging under the hulls may help.

On the jetty or marina you are at high risk of destruction from everything around you. Do as much as you can to reduce windage, secure lines, stop chafe and allow for the wide tidal ranges that occur during cyclones.

Trailerable multihulls should be towed away. Drop the rig, tie the trailer down and triple lash every line.

Beaching is an option in the unprotected bay. Read the chapter on Beaching and how to get your multihull ashore. Just being on the hard is not necessarily any better than on the water unless protection is found and the ability to secure to the earth increased.

DINGHY

The best dinghy is one that can be safely stowed away at sea, is accessible in an emergency, is capable of rowing out to set an anchor and is light enough to help keep the payload down.

There is plenty of deck storage area on a multihull although there are some traps.

Multihull Seamanship Rule:
Do not store a dinghy on trampoline netting when at sea.

This is especially true of forward trampoline netting. A decent wave, either over the top or from under the netting may take both trampoline and dinghy with it. The force behind a dinghy full of water travelling at speed is very high. Few trampolines will survive.

Towing a dinghy needs care. There is a wind tunnel effect on catamarans that flip lighter model dinghies. The wave pattern of both trimarans and catamarans also has an effect on the way a towed dinghy will ride. The dinghy painter needs to be long enough to adjust the tow length to place the dinghy in the best position in the wave pattern. Better still pull the dinghy aboard.

There is no ideal multihull dinghy. Weight is a consideration and the lighter the better. Conversely the dinghy should be stout enough to carry your heaviest anchor so that you can lay the anchor if grounded. This will enable winching your multihull free.

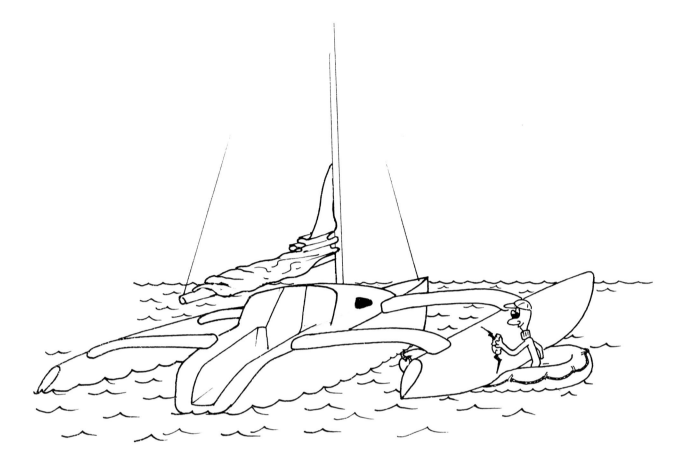

Many cruising multihulls have two dinghies - an inflatable which packs away and a sturdy work dinghy. Sailboards are easily stowed but avoid lashing them to guard rails in rough conditions. A good wave through the net may bend the rails and take the lot away. It is better to secure anything that has to stay on deck against hard deck.

Inflatable dinghies have the advantage of being able to be used under a float or hull (in calm conditions) to elevate it out of the water to effect repairs.

A dinghy is not a liferaft. It does not often have built in buoyancy, cover, water, food, flares, signalling mirror, fishing line or most importantly, rapid release and access either way up.

At anchor the dinghy will usually manage to find its way under a catamarans bridgedeck or the wing of a trimaran. If the painter goes under a trimarans high riding ama then the dinghy may even jam and sink. At best the stuck dinghy will wake you up from a blissful sleep. At worst it will damage hull sides and sometimes sink itself. Pull them on deck.

DISMASTING

Dismasting is an all too common occurrence on racing multihulls. Many of the problems arise from inadequate maintenance of the more flexible rigging systems. Rigid beam multihulls (bridgedeck catamarans) have much the same wear on rigging as monohulls. All other multihulls have a slack leeward stay when hard pressed to windward. This flexibility can fatigue the terminal points and the wire entry into the swages. It is important to have 'pressed' swages rather than 'rolled' swages. Pressed swages put an even load on all the wire strands. Rolled swaging can load up one side and increase the likelihood of a fatigue fracture.

Dismasting is a disaster that can quickly escalate into both a life threatening and a hull destroying situation.

Multihull Seamanship Rule:
Have a readily available system to cut the mast and rigging free.

If the mast falls over the float it may start to cut into the hull to the extent that it causes marked structural damage. In a large swell or wave action the damaged rig may endanger life as it swings across the hulls. Work fast to secure it or cut it free.

In some cases the mast can be salvaged if it remains attached to the boat. Secure it via a point that will not chafe the hulls.

Jury rigs work well on multihulls and are easily set up because of the wide beam. Unfortunately many multihulls no longer have a need for spinnaker poles because they use a permanently mounted bowsprit.

The options available for a jury mast include the boom, the forebeam pole, spliced dinghy oars, the rig from a sailboard or remnants of the original mast. It is a tough job without the right tools. For this reason alone it is essential that the survival pack contains a hacksaw (with spare blades), a bolt cutter and splicing material and enough adjustable wrenches to fit all the rigging bolts and nuts.

ELECTRICITY

Solar panels

Solar panels work better mounted on a platform that is adjustable to the angle of the sun. Unfortunately the sun moves and a multihull rarely faces the same direction for long. Never-the-less if most of your charging is done on the mooring then the best position can be calculated allowing for local wind directions, currents and sun angles.

Solar panels work poorly whenever a shadow or line is cast across their surface. The uncluttered bow and stern areas on floats or catamaran hulls are thus ideal for exposure but do not block access. This is also where you step aboard, run mooring lines and attach block systems. Solar panels do not have much in the way of a non-skid surface.

For intermittent solar panel use they can be mobile and need not be permanently mounted. There are flexible solar panels which are light and easily stored.

Wind generators

Wind generators work well when they are in a predictable upright position. The high apparent wind speed of a multihull also improves their performance. The windage and weight of wind generators reduces their popularity on racing multihulls and at high speeds they also produce a moderate noise.

Motor driven generators

Motor driven generators work as for other yachts. Many outboards now have a built in generator although the wiring of this is often an option. The output from an outboard generator is usually much less than that from an inboard engine. It is possible to run a water pick-up line for the cooling system on an outboard without putting the leg and propeller in the water. This way you can generate electricity without having to motor.

Portable generators are also available in lightweight models ranging from 350 volt amps upwards. Inboard diesel motors with generators are the most fuel efficient and capable of the high charging and power rates.

Circuitry

When wiring up a multihull consider the problems of longer distances to each bow and the flexibility of the beam structures. Any external wiring is subject to high spray levels. At the design stage good sized, lightweight conduit should be added to those areas not accessible such as through beam fairings. Use a wire core diameter that will carry the load without voltage drop.

Batteries

Batteries should be specifically designed into the multihull so they are firmly mounted and stored above the inverted waterline. The best batteries are sealed or gel types. All batteries give off hydrogen gas when being charged. The air around batteries must be vented away from sparks or flame. Sealed batteries also produce hydrogen and if charged too quickly may produce a problem in the battery with pressure build up. Consult the battery manufactures specifications. Sealed gel batteries are ideal for multihulls. Battery weight should be as central fore-and-aft and as low as possible i.e. In a catamaran in a sealed position in a float and in a trimaran in the centre of the main hull. If you are holed then be aware that the batteries could be immersed.

Battery immersion and chlorine

Chlorine is generated by running an electrical current through salt water. Fortunately copper (the main component of marine electrical wiring) and stainless steel do not generate chlorine at 12 volts. The copper quickly forms an insoluble coating and becomes non-reactive and stainless steel simply loses its passivity and dissolves slowly under the influence of a potential. The one metal that shows a tendency to produce chlorine is lead. The battery terminals are the main culprit.
Chlorine has the following effects:
1 ppm (part per million) = sick and pale.
3.5 ppm = odour detectable.
4 ppm = maximum level for 1 hour without serious consequences.
5 ppm = breathing affected in minutes.
15 ppm = throat irritation.

30 ppm = coughing.
40-60 ppm = life threatening in one hour.
1000 ppm = rapidly fatal.

From the above details it is obvious that if you can smell chlorine it is doing you harm.
The average marine battery with exposed terminals produces 4 ppm chlorine gas/cubic metre of air/minute.

How to avoid chlorine gas generation

Chlorine is produced mainly by battery terminals therefore avoid them coming in contact with sea water. This may be done by simply greasing the terminals regularly after the connections have been made or spraying them with a marine moisture repellent.
It is worth remembering that the current drawn by submerging an electrical circuit is small (around two amps) and hence it is possible to run a bilge pump or radio even if the batteries are submerged. A healthy battery with greased terminals will cope as long as no salt water leaks into the acid.

Multihull Seamanship Rule:
Use sealed gel batteries and always grease or coat the terminals regularly.

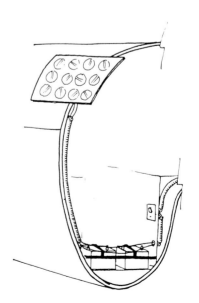

FIRE & GAS

Fire is a good argument for a liferaft. Most multihulls are flammable. Fire extinguishers need to be placed where they can be accessed quickly and without having to search in smoke or flame filled areas. Do not place the extinguishers in the galley or engine room. It is better to have them mounted near these areas, close to a hatch so that you can reach in and grab them.

A fire blanket is a cheap effective means of dousing a cooking fire. It also can be used to wrap a person in who is on fire.

Gas bottles should be in their own locker that ventilates externally. Bridgedeck catamarans have plenty of available space although do not get trapped into tucking the locker against a bulkhead where the natural slope is into the cabin.

Many racing multihulls use screw on disposable gas containers to save weight. Extra caution is needed with these as when the tops are pierced gas can escape momentarily. Do not use rusty containers.

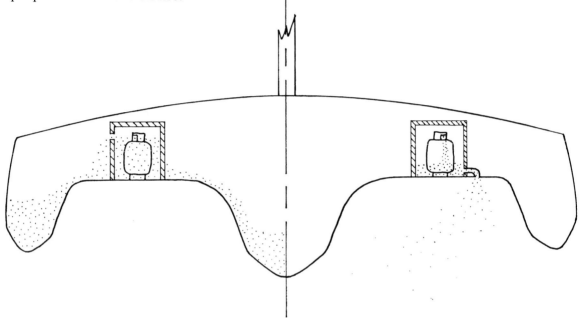

Gas explosions are all too common. One advantage of multihulls is that the bilges are shallow. A disadvantage is that you can have three bilges. If you have a gas leak immediately turn off the battery isolation switches and any flame source. Remember that gas is heavier than air and will filter into every corner of the floor. Open all hatches and start bailing the air from the floor out. A hand bilge pump will work to pump gas overboard also. Spend twice the length of time as you think you need in baling out. Do not use electric bilge pumps - they may spark.

Methylated spirits is probably the safest for cooking as it does not explode and can be extinguished with water. Some multihulls use a microwave oven with an inverter to convert 12 volt DC into 240 volt AC - or use a 240 volt generator.

Multihull Seamanship Rule:
Fire happens. If you have two hulls or more
have two extinguishers.

Fuel storage in a multihull is dependent on the type and quantity. Outboard petrol is usually in portable containers. Lash them down and ensure that likely fire sources are well clear. Do not store petrol in compartments with accommodation or cooking. Ideally store it in a separate ventilated compartment on deck.

If you have a considerable weight of fuel store it centrally and low. Long fuel lines are easily made but watch for leaks.

Multihull Seamanship Rule:
Check all fuel lines - gas and petrol -
regularly.

A flexing beam and an inflexible gas line can mean disaster.

FLARES & TORCHES

Do not store flares near any source of flame or likely fire area. This sounds obvious but many sailors like to keep out of date flares 'just in case'. If you intend to keep them have them stored in a spare watertight calamity pack in a position where they can be accessed. Loose flares in a locker are a recipe for disaster.

Multihull Seamanship Rule:
Keep a white flare near the helm.

A white flare is a powerful message to any vessel that is on a collision course with you and does not appear to be aware of your position or speed. Occasionally navigation lights fail. A torch at the helm and a white flare make good emergency back-ups. Catamarans with two cockpits and trimarans with three should have two or three sets of these respectively. Do not drip burning flare particles onto the deck. They are a big fire risk.

Every torch should have a lanyard and be waterproof.

At night the first thing overboard in a man-overboard situation should be a torch. A person in the water then can tell you where they are.

The best place to look for somebody in the water is from aloft or on the forward beam.

On a stable multihull you can safely get to the first spreader without the mast trying to sling you overboard. The helmsman has enough to do without trying to plug in a spotlight, turn on the power to the plug and stretch the leads to where the torch is needed.

The cost of torch batteries is insignificant when you are entering an unfamiliar river entrance at night. Always have a spare set for each torch.

Masthead strobe lights are not a legal addition but in emergency situations they are the brightest way of saying 'I am here'. Many standard tricolour and white masthead light fittings come with an optional strobe.

A portable strobe light is essential for on the danbuoy. A single white light does not work from such low levels without appearing to flash due to wave action. A strobe has the intensity and the pattern to attract attention. Lashed on the end of the extendible boat hook it can be raised as needed.

Multihull Seamanship Rule:
Always carry an accessible portable strobe.

GUSTY CONDITIONS

Gusty conditions can be treacherous to safe multihull sailing if you are not prepared for them. There are a few rules which will reduce the risk of capsize.

Multihull Seamanship Rule:
Do not carry too much sail in gusty wind.

If the wind strength is rapidly fluctuating or changing direction reef as you would for the maximum wind speed in the gusts.

A smart sailor knows what sail is needed in what wind strengths. It is possible to construct a sail area/wind strength chart - as long as you have the ability to accurately determine the wind strength. Do not get tricked into reefing for the apparent wind only. Downwind this can be disastrous when you round up to head to windward.

Windward gust control

When overpowered by a gust immediately ease (or dump) the traveller and/or mainsheet. Be aware that the relative increased power on the headsail will want to drive the yacht downwind so round up slowly and in control.

Downwind gust control

Sail area is critical. Never carry too much sail. If you think you need to reef then reef.

When overpowered in a gust the correct action is to bear away and ease the sheets. Never luff up as this increases the apparent wind speed. By bearing away you effectively reduce the apparent wind and ease the pressure on the sails. As soon as the gust passes it's time to reef.

Multihull Seamanship Rule:
When hit by a gust when sailing downwind bear away, ease sheets and run with it.

IN IRONS

Although not unique to multihulls, getting caught 'in irons' is a lot more common. 'In irons' is the state of stalling when the multihull has attempted to tack or has pointed so high into the wind that all forward motion is lost and the multihull starts to drift backwards.

Multihull Seamanship Rule
To get out of 'irons' release the headsail, push the rudder(s) over and the boom away so the multihull sails backwards and around onto the tack required.

It is possible to manoeuvre backwards with considerable skill. As soon as the mainsail has wind coming on it from the windward side, sheet in the headsail, correct the helm and sheet in the main as you progress forward. Be aware that you will have considerable leeway (sideways drift) until you get under way.

All steering systems should have a rudder lock that stops the rudders riding into a position where they may be damaged or the steering system stressed.

How not to get caught in irons

When initiating a tack ensure your multihull has enough momentum to go through the eye of the wind. If your multihull has a high aspect main and a non-overlapping headsail then it may be necessary to release the mainsail so that it does not power on until the headsail fills on the opposite tack. If momentum is minimal then the headsail may need to be backed first to blow the bow further around.

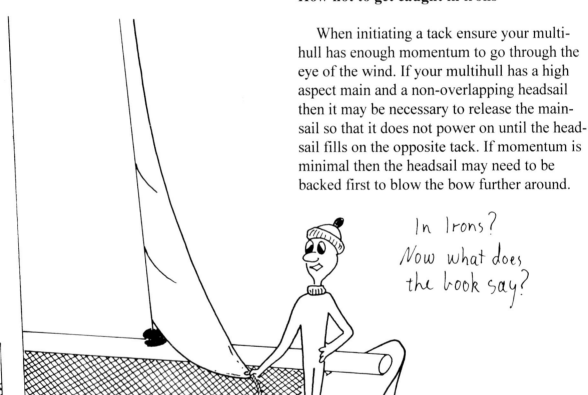

In Irons?
Now what does
the book say?

JETTY WORK

Handling and docking a multihull is an acquired skill.

Multihull Seamanship Rule:
Practise manoeuvring in open spaces.

The ease with which a multihull is moved by the wind has a major influence on the approach to a jetty. The lighter the multihull and the larger the windage (e.g. wing masts) the more preparation is required. Catamarans with twin diesel inboards have excellent manoeuvrability. In contrast a single stern mounted outboard requires a lot of careful forethought.

Single outboard driven multihulls

Many multihulls need to be going about four knots before they will turn sharply into the wind by rudder action lone. It is an advantage to be able to steer the outboard to manoeuvre when a multihull is not moving fast enough for the rudders to have much effect.

If the wind is light you will have better manoeuvrability with the centreboard(s) up. If the wind is strong enough to cause side slipping or leeway then centreboard(s) down will help reduce this at the cost of a slightly wider steering circle.

Lines and fenders should be prepared well in advance. When approaching a jetty to windward have someone ready to secure a line from the bow and use reverse to swing the stern in. On a trimaran have the crewman on the middle hull with the line secured to the float.

When leaving a jetty think ahead about the effect of the wind. Leave a line secured to the jetty to facilitate turning if the room is tight. To ensure the line will run free never have it spliced at the end. A splice will mean a thicker portion of rope and one day it will catch on a bollard or jetty structure.

Twin motor manoeuvring

If both propellers rotate in the same direction then be aware of the significant sideways pull when the motors are given short hard thrusts. By using this knowledge it is often easier to come alongside a jetty in one particular direction. If the propellers are counter rotating (i.e.drive in opposite directions) then this will not occur and coming into a jetty will require large movements of the rudders to direct water flow over the rudders to steer the stern.

Practice your approach technique when mooring up in tight areas. You need to be able to extend your 'feel' to all corners of the multihull so the width is well covered. When going into a marina berth concentrate on one hull, getting it as close as possible. Occasionally watch the fit of the other hull but if your preparation is right then only one hull needs to be parked correctly - the other will follow!

Fenders

Most multihulls have straight sides so fenders are needed along the length. If the jetty consists only of posts then rubbing boards should be used. On trimaran floats the fenders need to have ties top and bottom so they can be tied around the float. This is especially true if the floats are capable of riding up in bouncing waves.

If the springs are run from amidships (as is often incorrectly done) then the bow and stern can swing and the tensioning effect is lost. Always allow for the tide. The jetty is not the place to fly a hull.

Multihull Seamanship Rule:
If in doubt when approaching a jetty do a false run to test windage and current.

Mooring up

Tie up your multihull correctly. Many trimarans do not have cleats on the outer floats and the lines have to be run inboard. There are four lines needed. The head rope and the stern rope should run from the bow and stern away from the boat at about 45 degrees to the quay. This will allow for tidal range. Springs should always be rigged from the bow and the stern and should run at least the length of the hull. The springers should be as tight as possible. This will ensure the hulls cannot rotate to damage the bow or transoms.

Chafe is a major mooring problem. Protect lines running over jetty boards with hose. Look at the fairleads, rigging and deck fittings for potential chafe points.

When tying up tie a knot that can be undone. Multihulls with a high windage work their mooring lines heavily and a bowline reduces the strength of the rope by about 50 percent and can be impossible to untie when under strain. It is better to use a round turn and two half hitches. This will not jam under strain, it grips the object tightly (thus not suffering as much chafe) and will not slip or spring apart.

Always use four separate lines for mooring up. If the one line is used for a spring and a head or stern rope then adjustment cannot be done without interfering with others. Ideally each line also should have its own cleat.

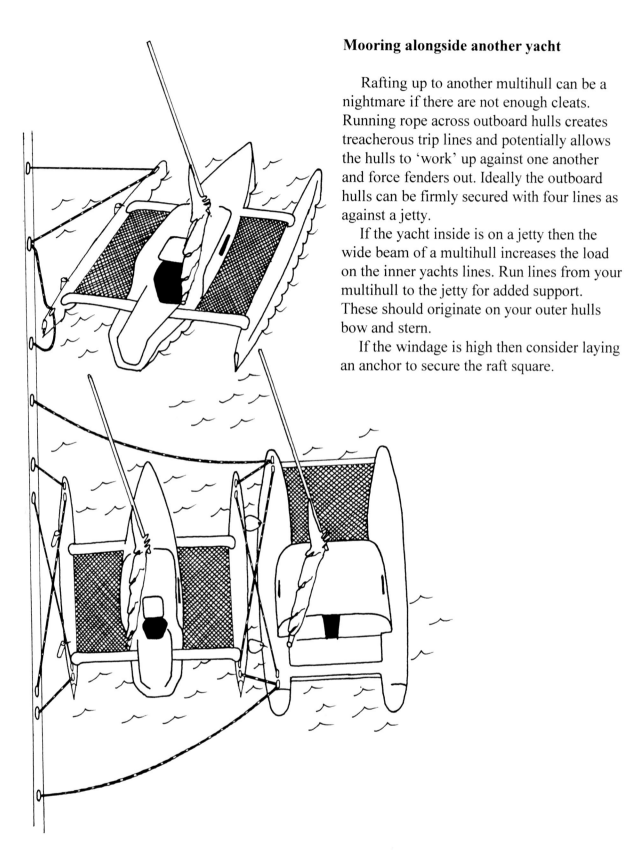

Mooring alongside another yacht

Rafting up to another multihull can be a nightmare if there are not enough cleats. Running rope across outboard hulls creates treacherous trip lines and potentially allows the hulls to 'work' up against one another and force fenders out. Ideally the outboard hulls can be firmly secured with four lines as against a jetty.

If the yacht inside is on a jetty then the wide beam of a multihull increases the load on the inner yachts lines. Run lines from your multihull to the jetty for added support. These should originate on your outer hulls bow and stern.

If the windage is high then consider laying an anchor to secure the raft square.

Beam wind jetty handling

One of the more awkward manoeuvres is leaving a jetty with a beam wind pushing your multihull onto it. There are two techniques depending on how many motors you have.

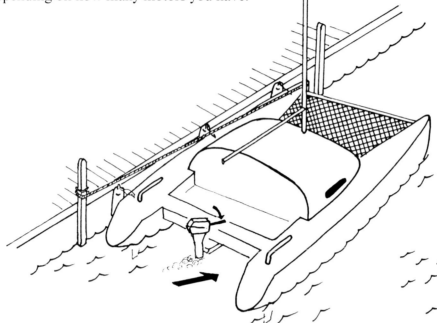

• Catamarans and Trimarans with central motors.

If possible angle the drive force so that the side force of the propeller is combined with the spring line. When the multihulls stern is clear in the channel drive in reverse to leave the jetty.

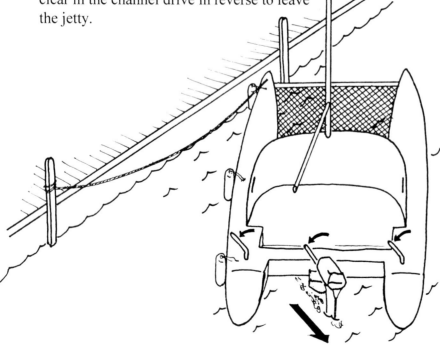

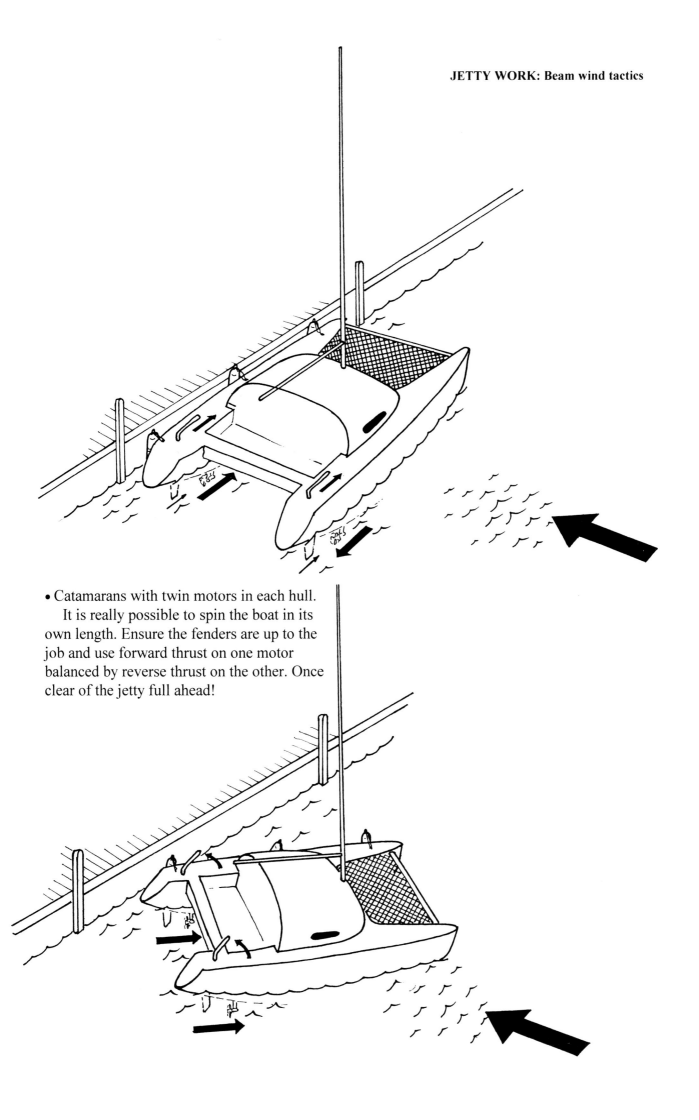

• Catamarans with twin motors in each hull.
It is really possible to spin the boat in its
own length. Ensure the fenders are up to the
job and use forward thrust on one motor
balanced by reverse thrust on the other. Once
clear of the jetty full ahead!

LIFERAFTS

Some multihull sailors say they do not need to carry a liferaft because their multihull cannot sink. A multihull surfing down the face of a wave and hitting an immobile humpback whale does not sink. It just breaks into little pieces. Liferafts are a back-up. Stay with your multihull until there is nothing left.

Multihull Seamanship Rule:
Only ever step up into a liferaft.

Destruction can occur through impact or fire. A dinghy is useful but it is not a liferaft. A dinghy will not have automatic carbon dioxide inflation, automatic canopy, water, ballast bags or survival equipment. Human nature will usually ensure that the dinghy has been previously used and something will be missing or broken.

Positioning of a liferaft on a multihull needs careful thought. It needs to be accessed from both the upright and capsized position. This can be as simple as having it tied to the trampoline netting with a knife lashed and taped on both sides. It could also be stored in a locker that is accessed in both positions. If you are having a yacht designed or built then this is the best time to arrange liferaft stowage. Too many multihulls stow the liferaft as an afterthought and it ends up in an exposed position where wind driven salt or rain water can slowly penetrate the raft and shorten its life.

Liferafts come in soft and hard packs. Soft packs are lighter but less weather resistant unless the actual raft is vacuum sealed and completely watertight. The type of pack you need is very much dependent on the storage position. An advantage of soft valise packs is that they are more readily passed through an escape hatch if stored inboard.

The use of a liferaft on a capsized multihull needs careful thought. Liferafts, once inflated, are easily damaged if not tethered correctly. The raft should only be inflated if absolutely necessary.

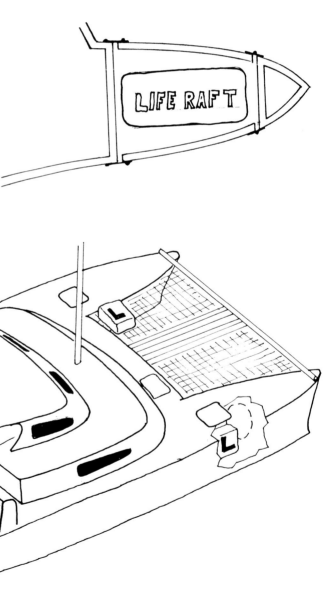

LIGHTNING

Lightning is a real problem on every yacht. Over 10 percent of all fatalities on cruising yachts are from lightning strikes. Most marine authorities lay down recommendations for lightning protection but very few multihull (and other yacht) sailors adhere to them. There are a few lightning problems specific to multihulls. First a general overview about the problem.

Lightning is a multidirectional flow of charges exceeding 200,000 amperes at over 30,000 degrees Celsius for a matter of milliseconds. Clouds with strong updraughts and downdrafts generate high electrical charges. When these charges reach a high enough level then cloud to ground or cloud to cloud discharges occur.

The area of most lightning strikes is under the dark area of a cumulo nimbus storm system. First you will be hit by the increased wind turbulence, then a rain area before entering the dark high risk lightning zone. As the storm cell moves along the secondary rain area at the back of the system may announce your exit from the higher risk area.

Lightning protection systems

Lightning usually strikes the highest point and takes the path of least electrical resistance to ground. In the ideal situation this route is via a mast spike (a copper rod with a pointed end) through a sufficient cross sectioned purpose placed cable to a large, separate ground plate. The spike should be at least 15 cm above other masthead equipment (including VHF aerials).

The grounding for multihulls

Aluminium multihulls can ground via connecting the mast base or mast step to the hull metal with a large, low resistance bonding strap.

Wooden or fibreglass multihulls need a large separate ground shoe. Never bond the lightning system to machinery, electrical system negatives, radio earth plates or any bronze through hull systems.

Emergency ground

Clamp a heavy gauge copper cable to about half a metre of stay. The other end should be clamped to a ground plate and hung in the water. Chains and anchors are ineffective.

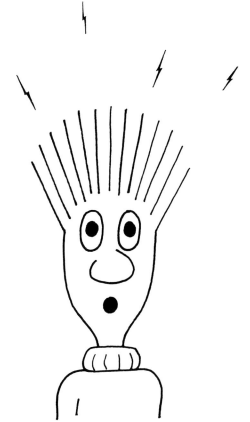

Lightning safety

Stay in the hulls or bridgedeck cabin.

Avoid all metal mast fittings including the mast compression post and chainplates

If struck by lightning without adequate protection you will probably lose all electronics. Take down your position, bearing and speed at regular intervals during electrical storms.

Turn off all electronic equipment, isolate them if possible. Disconnect aerials.

Do not operate radios unless in extreme emergency. A hand held VHF is a great back-up should lightning blow all electronics.

After a lightning strike.

Your compass may be incorrect. It should be swung (tested for error on all points) before being used for safe navigation.

Check all running rigging and fittings.

Check all through hull fittings - especially chainplates, log fittings and stern glands.

MAN OVERBOARD

Man overboard prevention

Lifelines do not stop people falling off. If you are the only one on deck wear a safety harness in all conditions.

Multihull Seamanship Rule:
One hand for the boat.

Multihulls accelerate and turn quickly, causing the unwary to lose balance. Toe lines around the edge (height 25 mm minimum), lifelines (height 600 mm minimum, gap 380 mm maximum), good non-slip (where it is needed) and well placed hand holds all help moving about safely.

The leeward stays are often loose - especially if your multihull has a rotating mast. Do not use this for support.

Multihulls move quickly. Wear a safety harness and connect the lifeline when on deck.

What to do if the man overboard is visible.

Multihull Seamanship Rule:
Man overboard then S.T.O.P.

S = Stop. Round up and back sails.
T = Throw a lifebuoy and strobe.
O = Observe. Delegate someone to watch.
P = Prepare to lift person aboard.

Man overboard while beating or reaching

Tack instantly and keep headsail aback. Shout 'man overboard' and have one person pointing to the person in the water. If you are drifting away from the person then deploy the day-buoy. If you are drifting toward them get the heaving lines ready.

Ensure all the crew have their harnesses and life lines on before preparing to haul the person aboard.

If you do not drift down onto the person then you should determine the best way for your multihull to approach. A racing yacht may find it easier to start the motor, drop the mainsail and circle to approach from leeward. Have your retrieval system prepared in advance. If you keep sails up, release the headsail and approach from downwind so the person is visible to the helmsman. Be aware that as you slow to pick up the crewman leeway increases rapidly. Towing a long (e.g. 80 metre) retrieval sling and rounding the person in a tight circle is one technique for getting them attached.

Man overboard on a spinnaker run

Drop the danbuoy immediately. Shout 'man overboard' and have one person pointing at the person in the water. Smoke the spinnaker halyard then round up and stop the boat. Stuff the spinnaker down the hatch and organise the sheets (you don't want sheets under the rudder or around the propellers). Approach the man overboard from leeward and retrieve.

If you are the one overboard then...

Look for the danbuoy and swim to it.

Clip yourself into the life ring. Minimise heat loss by keeping your armpits close to your body, legs lifted toward your chest.

Retrieve the whistle (and light if it is night) from pockets.

Catch the heaving line or grab the line that should be permanently under the crossarms.

Watch for a trailing lifering being towed behind the yacht.

Make your way to the stern of the multihull where it is easy to get aboard.

Self sufficiency after falling overboard

You can increase your chances of being found and surviving if you have the following:
- Inflatable vest
- Wrist strobe
- Pocket pea-less whistle (these work after being submerged)
- Pocket flare
- Sea marker dye

Retrieval of the man overboard

Lifting a person onto a multihull has some problems. The floats on a trimaran may be airborne and slam down onto the person in the water. If this is the case then lift them onto the central hull, preferably on the windward side.

Many multihulls have steps on the stern making life much easier.

If the person is unconscious or unable to climb then there are many methods to help them aboard. Harness systems or lifejackets or chest lines attached to a halyard are readily available methods. Check that your halyards make it to the water. If not have a spare line ready with the sling or harness stored in the cockpit for 'man overboard' situations.

75

If the man overboard is not visible

Again STOP.

Drop a marker overboard e.g. lifering or lifejacket.

Plot position and time the person was last sighted. Many global positioning satellite (GPS) navigation units have a button to instantly record your position.

Record yacht speed, heading and course over which you have travelled since the person was last seen.

Send distress signals to facilitate the search by other vessels or planes in the area. Time is critical.

Gybe and crisscross, broad reaching over your previous route. If you are likely to travel too fast, then drop the mainsail and gybe downwind under headsail alone.

Manoeuvring toward the man overboard

The major problem is that multihulls are more affected by drift and windage at low speeds. A line towed astern may drag the person along, further weakening them and dragging them under. If they are in a sling or lifering get them to face backwards and shorten the line as soon as the person is attached.

Multihulls also lose way very quickly in any chop. Have motor power ready to help hold station.

Of all the seamanship safety techniques that should be practised the man overboard recovery is the most important. Every multihull differs in its speed, layout of equipment, manoeuvrability and drift. Practice on a regular basis the recovery of an object as quickly as possible. Time yourself and your crew.

MASTS

Going aloft

The motion of a multihull mast has both advantages and disadvantages when it has to be climbed. At sea this is a potentially dangerous exercise. The mast, although remaining mainly upright, is prone to rapid movements in any direction as the multihull goes over waves.

Try to avoid going aloft. Have a spare halyard available for headsails. Regularly service blocks and sheaves so the risk of a wire halyard jumping a sheave and jamming is reduced.

If you have to go aloft prepare well first.

Multihull Seamanship Rule:
If you have to go aloft at sea, sail in a direction that has the least jarring motion.

Downwind is usually the best. Have all tools held by a lanyard. Secure the bosuns chair with D Shackles - not snap shackles. A safety harness and lifeline is needed as a back-up to the halyard. At every opportunity secure yourself to minimise any drop. Use a harness line with three attachment points so you are never unattached.

Pad your body well with jumpers, tracksuits and a helmet if you have one. Stuff numerous towels down your pants as the crutch is a prime injury point. Assist the person winching you aloft by hauling yourself where possible. Always hold on by two hands until at the level where you need to work. Wing masts make it difficult to grip the mast with your legs so wedge yourself firmly against any rigging and work quickly.

Before any offshore trip, do a run up the mast and check out the rig and your climbing gear.

If you have to go aloft and you are sailing solo, then plan the sequence carefully.

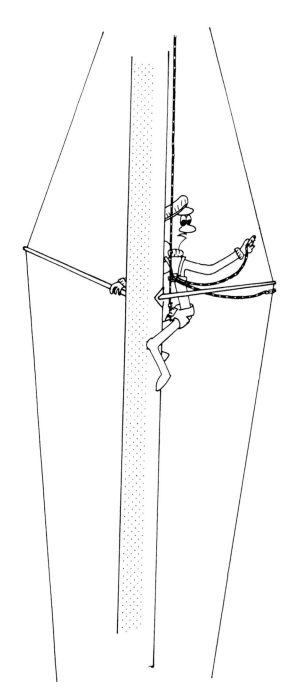

You will need a four-to-one purchase system and a bag on the bosuns chair to catch the tail of the rope as you climb. If you don't catch the tail, it will probably tangle somewhere and leave you dangling alone up the mast.

Mast steps

Mast steps are suitable for in harbour use only. They must be used in conjunction with a safety harness and line. The line should have three attachment points - you and two for the rig - so that you are never not connected.

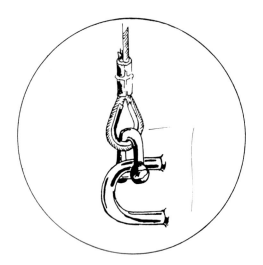

Rotating masts

A rotating mast increases the rig efficiency. The mast presents less drag at sea and on the mooring and they can be amateur built. There are various grades of rotating rigs. At one end of the spectrum are the wing sails, a total aerofoil section with little or no soft sail. In the middle are wing masts, having a large fore and aft length. When these are scaled down to a size that is manageable in a gale (e.g. mast area less than 10 percent of the total sail area) then the term rotating mast is aptly applied.

The danger point of a rotating mast is the mast spanner. During a tack or gybe, if the spanner is not released, when it does fly free it may smash the ankle of someone standing adjacent.

If the mast spanner (the rotation control) is not released during a tack the sails may be damaged by the diamonds.

Always do a regular check on the attachment point of the three stays. This is an area of high load and should be heavily reinforced.

78

Multihull Seamanship Rule:
Check the rig by going aloft after each gale
and before sailing offshore.

The leeward stay is often slack on a
rotating rig. Have an elastic cord secured from
each sidestay to the deck a few metres up so it
does not whip about and increase the fatigue
at the turnbuckle or wire attachment.

Multihull Seamanship Rule:
Scan the rigging before each tack.

On a rotating rig there is a higher chance
that running backstays will be caught around
a spreader. Tacking will pull the spreader arm
off. A glance skyward will reduce the risk of a
problem. At night use a torch.

Rotating wing masts must be set up
perfectly to work better than a fixed rig. There
is more work required to get that
improvement in performance. Because a
rotating wing mast causes some increased
windage and 'sailing' on moorings, they are
not ideal for cruising multihulls.

Masthead tricolour lights

Masthead navigation lights do not work
on a rotating rig. A solution is to fit two
masthead tricolour lights, one for port tack
and the other for starboard tack. After
tacking, turn one off and the other on.

If you have your navigation lights
mounted on the hulls, then an all round white
light (designed for when at anchor) will
signify your presence when at sea in an
emergency. So will shining the spotlight on
the sails and turning on all cabin lights. If all
else fails try a white flare.

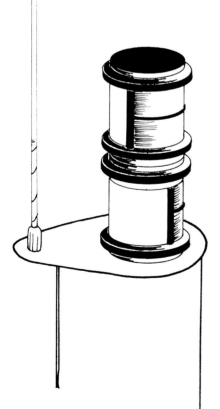

Conventional masts

Multihulls do not spill the wind when hit by a gust so the mast should be strong enough for the loads generated. Ensure your rigger is aware of this. Spreaders are needed if the stays are not separated wide on the beam. If the stays are spaced outboard on a rigid beam multihull (such as a bridgedeck catamaran) then spreaders can be done without. If the beam has any flexibility, then a series of short spreaders and a single cap shroud is a better arrangement. The mast then remains stiff if there is any movement in the beam.

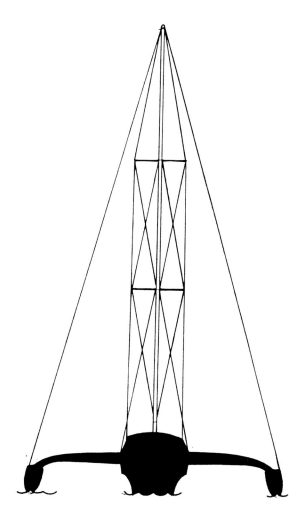

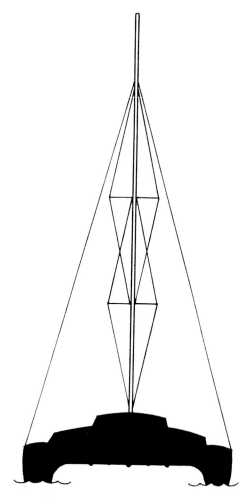

Unconventional masts

There are a few experimental rigs e.g. freestanding, rotating aerofoils and solid wing sails. The seamanship characteristics of these are unique and the exponents of the sail/rig in question should be contacted if you are interested.

MOTORS

Outboard motors

The light weight and long narrow hulls of a multihull are easily driven. For these reasons outboards are popular. The advantages of outboards on multihulls include ease of servicing access, lighter weight, manoeuvrability if steerable and initial cost. The disadvantages are exposure to the elements, weight at end of hulls, potential propeller ventilation, high fuel consumption and fuel flammability.

There are solutions to the above disadvantages. Mount the outboard as far forward as possible and reduce the exposure to spray by building protective barriers e.g. on a trimarans back beam alongside the central hull.

Fuel flammability is lessened if shut off valves are close to the motor and the tank and all fuel lines fire resistant. Ensure portable fuel tanks are not near gas bottles.

Position the outboard motor so it can be placed in the water and started without any crew member having to be substantially outside either the pushpit, guard rails or lifelines. An alternative if this is not possible is to only operate the outboard while wearing a safety harness.

Extra long shafts should be used to put the propeller as far under the water as possible. As the stern lifts clear of the water air may be sucked down to the propeller causing ventilation and loss of drive.

Ensure the motor and propeller are appropriate for the cruising speed and load of the multihull.

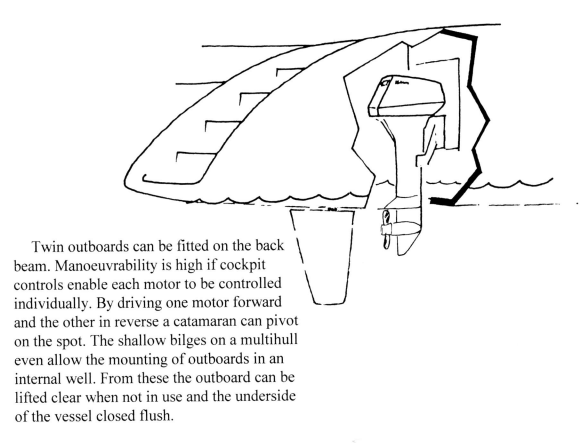

Twin outboards can be fitted on the back beam. Manoeuvrability is high if cockpit controls enable each motor to be controlled individually. By driving one motor forward and the other in reverse a catamaran can pivot on the spot. The shallow bilges on a multihull even allow the mounting of outboards in an internal well. From these the outboard can be lifted clear when not in use and the underside of the vessel closed flush.

Standard outboards have small, high speed propellers that produce very low thrust at yacht speeds. Special high thrust yacht auxiliary outboards are far superior although beware of some 'yacht' outboards which may not be ideal because of the ease with which the hulls are driven. Many motors are designed for heavy displacement vessels.

The ability of an outboard to pull up your multihull in reverse is dependent on the propeller function. Reverse exhausting propellers are more efficient in reverse than standard propellers.

Mounting a single diesel in a catamaran can work by either positioning it in central nacelle (with a drop down outboard leg) or in one hull. The off-centre motor still works well although manoeuvrability requires practice. Twin, inboard diesels give excellent control in tight situations.

The drag from a permanently mounted propeller increases with increasing boat speed under sail. If you are serious about performance then incorporate a folding or feathering propeller. Either way some protection will need to be made so the propeller is not the first thing to hit bottom. A small skeg will make a difference.

Inboard motors

Diesel inboard motors are lighter and more powerful than in years past. They need only 30% of the fuel store of a two stroke petrol motor or 60% of a four stroke petrol motor for the same work. They have the advantage of being able to provide power for generators and refrigeration.

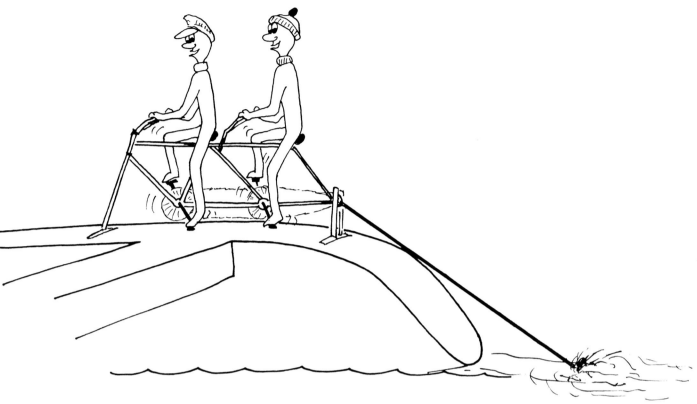

Manpower

There are times when you may need to move your multihull under your own muscle. If you only have dinghy oars then rowing works. Expect to have a maximum rate of 1 -2 knots in very light conditions and only be able to maintain this for an hour or so per rower. Should your multihull be fitted with long rowing oars then these can be mounted on the sidestays and by walking backwards and forwards give an extra half knot. If only one sculling oar is on board then sculling off the back beam works also.

If you are in a race that allows man-driven power then a most efficient device is a propeller that is chain driven and geared onto a tandem bicycle. Paddling using small paddles is almost useless.

RACING SEAMANSHIP

There are a number of seamanship features of multihulls that only become a concern in the racing environment. Every other chapter in this book is relevant to the racing multihull but none more so than capsize risk.

The majority of multihulls that capsize do so while racing in winds around 30 to 40 knots true. Squalls and rogue waves are the environmental triggers but there are a number of other factors involved depending on the sailing angle.

rapidly. Downwind the mainsail power is not as easily able to be dumped by releasing sheets or traveller.

The danger situation is when surfing and the bows bury into the wave ahead, stalling the multihull and dramatically increasing the apparent wind force.

Racing downwind

The large roach, high aspect multihull mainsail has a lot of power and can cause the capsize of a multihull. This capsize effect is increased in fractional rigged multihulls due to them carrying relatively higher masts.

Multihull Seamanship Rule:
Reef the mainsail if surfing is occurring.

You will still surf under the power of the spinnaker. The spinnaker sheets should be able to be quickly released and power lost

Wind power (force) increases to the square of the wind speed. This means that going from a wind of 10 knots apparent to 30 knots apparent increases the force on the sails nine times.

When surfing, a multihulls top speed can be limited by the towing of a drogue or anchor warp and chain. It is possible to tow a drogue while sailing under mainsail and spinnaker. The right set-up can allow constant sailing at 15 - 20 knots and become rate-limiting by increasing the drag at higher speeds i.e. no excessive surfing and thus no bow burying.

When racing you need to know the designed displacement of your multihull. Do not overload it. An overloaded multihull usually needs more sail to get it up to speed and accelerates slower. Therefore when it stalls downwind the wind force is higher as recovery is slower.

Trim is an important feature in burying the bows. Weight should never be moved forward to increase the ability to surf. Weight forward increases the risk of nose-diving into the wave ahead. Altering trim may be illegal under race rules. A racing seamanship feature would be to have the multihull trimmed to surf with the weight as far aft as possible. Ensure any heavy loads are well secured. An outboard motor on the hull floor or loose water containers increase the capsize force if they slide forward.

Skipper and crew fatigue is higher in the racing situation. At all times a sharp crewman should be responsible for seamanship decisions.

Multihull Seamanship Rule:
If you think a safety thought - do it.

Remember that mistakes are often made toward the end of a watch or the end of a stint on the helm. A surprising number of accidents occur within sight of the finish line or home port.

Speed downwind is achieved through utilising the high apparent wind a multihull generates.

Most multihulls develop a higher velocity made good (VMG) downwind if they gybe down the course rather than run square.

When racing downwind try and carry the wind angle from abeam. To do this round up enough to accelerate and 'bend' the wind forward then gently bear away and carry the altered apparent wind with you.

Racing upwind

Remember that the wind force increases to the square of the wind speed. On a multihull a small difference in wind speed dramatically changes boat speed. At lower wind speeds this means all effort should be made to find the wind slots and stick to them. As light winds vary in direction there is an optimum change that means you should tack. On most multihulls tacking loses momentum and takes time to get back to boat speed. In continuously varying wind directions a minimum of 10 degrees wind variation is usually needed to justify tacking.

Static capsize risk is the force required to turn a multihull over due to wind action alone. In gusty wind conditions be aware of the increased static capsize risk. Reef to the gust strength not to the average wind strength.

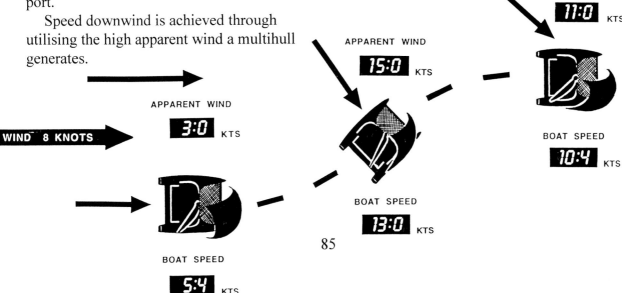

WIND 8 KNOTS

APPARENT WIND
3:0 KTS

BOAT SPEED
5:4 KTS

APPARENT WIND
15:0 KTS

BOAT SPEED
13:0 KTS

APPARENT WIND
11:0 KTS

BOAT SPEED
10:4 KTS

85

RADAR & RADAR REFLECTORS

Radar works well on a multihull because of the minimal heeling. If mounted on a rotating mast then a correction device is needed to allow for the rotation angle.

Radar should not be mounted too high nor too low. With height the pitching is increased and the radar will not detect low level targets e.g. coral reefs or breaking waves. A 16 mile radar needs only to be four metres above sea level. If lower than four metres the beam can cause medical problems as they work on microwaves (similar to a microwave oven). Some multihulls mount the radar on a stern support post. This stops any turbulent flow onto the mainsail but at the cost of exposing the radar dome to increased salt spray. The support posts should be as aerodynamic as possible.

Multihull Seamanship Rule:
Carry two radar reflectors - one on the mast, one in the calamity pack.

Radar reflectors

Have a portable radar reflector in the calamity pack. A mast, even an aluminium wing mast, is a poor radar reflector. A correctly designed and mounted radar reflector is necessary. These should be mounted as high as possible in the rigging. The design of the radar reflector for a multihull needs two characteristics - to be light and have low windage.

Many fishing boats and ships run radar continuously. A mastless or capsized multihull could aid discovery by running a radar reflector as high as possible on a jury mast. There are a number of options. A collapsible radar reflector could be stowed in the calamity pack. There are helium inflatable radar reflector balloons and a radar reflector kite available commercially.

Aluminium wine bladders are nearly useless as a reflector. Do not rely on them. Test data is available for radar reflectors. Make sure you have one that actually works.

RIGGING & ROPES

A multihull mast needs to withstand high loads. Because there is minimal heeling the stresses are greater than on an equivalent monohull rig.

Multihull Seamanship Rule:
Use a rigger who has multihull experience.

The wide stay base, due to a multihulls beam, allows for a more efficient shroud angle. If the beams are flexible then this must be accounted for.

Conventional spreader rigs are used on multihulls where crossbeam flexibility makes it impossible to attach the shrouds outboard. (e.g. some trimarans). They also allow overlapping headsails to be used.

Conventional masts also can be used without spreaders by leading the shrouds outboard. This is best on bridgedeck catamarans with their wide beam and greater structural stiffness. Alternatively double or triple diamonds can be incorporated with a single 3/4 shroud. The mast then remains stiff despite a small degree of flexing of the beams. This also allows overlapping headsails to be used.

To hold the rig up with only three shrouds from a single point requires an increased mast section size. Making the section aerodynamically efficient reduces drag and has the advantage of allowing a reduced sail plan. The rig windage is less at anchor and at sea. Rotating masts are another option.

Correct design and maintenance is needed to ensure the mast base rotates easily. The take-off point on the mast needs regular maintenance to ensure loads are taken evenly. Rotating masts impose greater flexing and fatigue on the wires leading to shorter wire life.

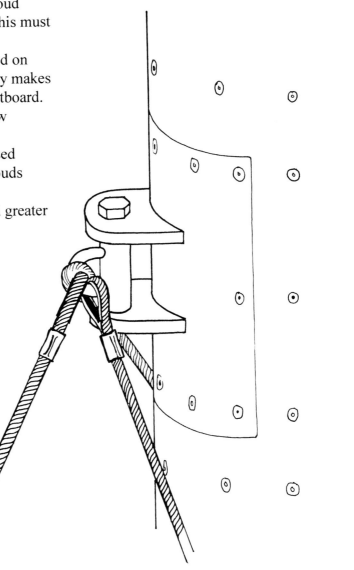

87

Regular rigging checks should be carried out to detect flex fractures. This is particularly true of the sidestay and seagull striker attachment points. Look carefully where the wire swage attaches to the wire of the turnbuckles. This is the point where many 19 strand wires start to break a strand or two.

Multihull Seamanship Rule:
You only see rigging that you look at. Climb the mast.

Before and after major voyages or races go up the mast and check everything.

The running rigging (sheet ropes, braces, halyards and backstay lines) all need maintenance and care. The two big destroyers of rope are sunlight and salt crystals. Both work to break down the fibre structure gradually. The loads are high on multihull running rigging because there is less 'give' when the yacht is hit by a gust. The force is converted into boat speed directly through the rigging.

Unused ropes should be bagged and protected from sunlight. When the opportunity arises rinse out all sheets and lines with fresh water to reduce the salt content.

Rope halyards should be regularly altered in length i.e. reversed or tied at a different level. This will reduce the point loading effect where they go through blocks and sheaves and help the ropes to last longer.

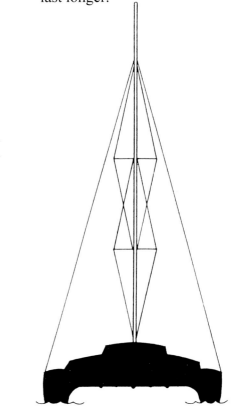

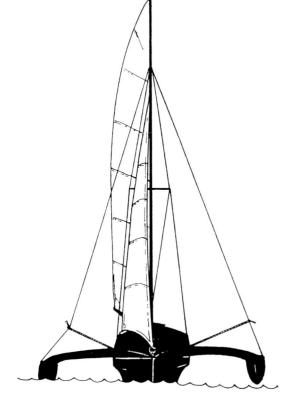

RIGHTING

No multihull self rights. They need assistance.

Multihull Seamanship Rule:
Know your options when organising to right a capsized multihull.

Crew-only righting

Righting a capsized multihull using only the crew is possible - it is done on off the beach multihulls every day.

There are many techniques that designers and owners have set up but few that have been used or tested in-situ.

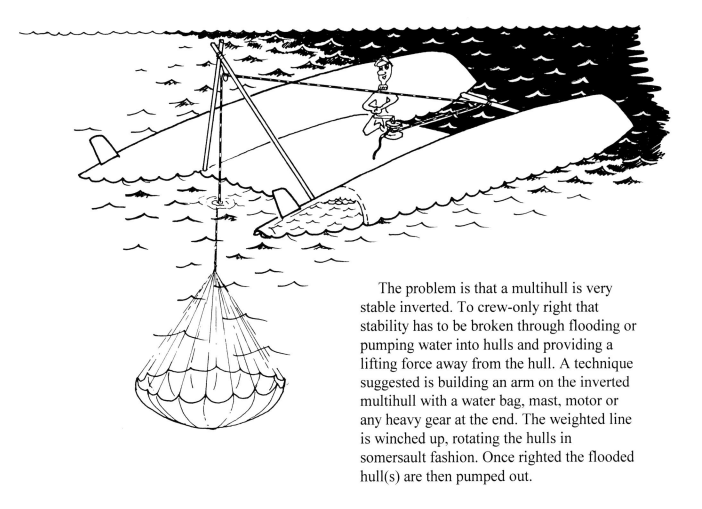

The problem is that a multihull is very stable inverted. To crew-only right that stability has to be broken through flooding or pumping water into hulls and providing a lifting force away from the hull. A technique suggested is building an arm on the inverted multihull with a water bag, mast, motor or any heavy gear at the end. The weighted line is winched up, rotating the hulls in somersault fashion. Once righted the flooded hull(s) are then pumped out.

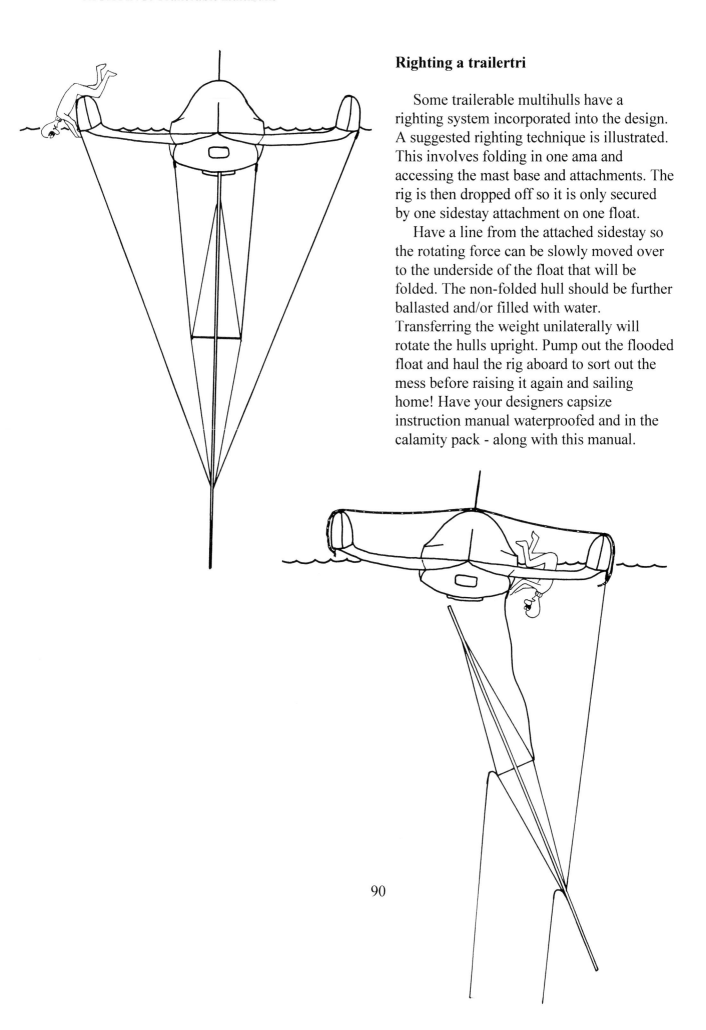

Righting a trailertri

Some trailerable multihulls have a righting system incorporated into the design. A suggested righting technique is illustrated. This involves folding in one ama and accessing the mast base and attachments. The rig is then dropped off so it is only secured by one sidestay attachment on one float.

Have a line from the attached sidestay so the rotating force can be slowly moved over to the underside of the float that will be folded. The non-folded hull should be further ballasted and/or filled with water. Transferring the weight unilaterally will rotate the hulls upright. Pump out the flooded float and haul the rig aboard to sort out the mess before raising it again and sailing home! Have your designers capsize instruction manual waterproofed and in the calamity pack - along with this manual.

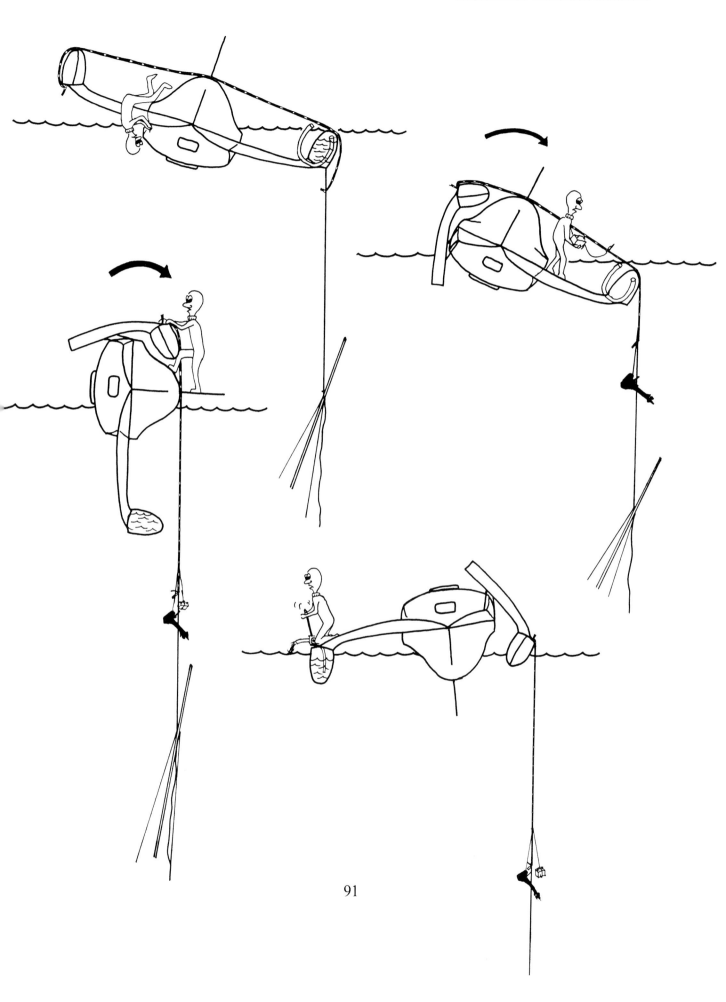

Assisted righting

Assisted righting at sea is achieved best by towing most multihulls end over end. The many attempts to pull them over sideways or crane them over from ships have usually resulted in substantial damage to the yachts due to the heavy loads on attachment points from the flooded hulls.

The tow-over technique is as follows. Look at the profile of the capsized multihull. Is there an end that is lower in the water? If there is then this is the end to try and drive under the water.

Attach strong lines to the higher end and run these back over the inverted hulls to a bridle point near the stern of the tow vessel. Steady towing will sink the lower end and the multihull will roll upright end over end.

The closer the tow vessel is to the inverted multihull the greater the effect of the propeller blast in assisting the rotation.

Many problems can occur at this stage. Some are design specific and what follows are ideas that might help.

If the mast remains intact then you may have to tow driving the stern of the multihull under. If the sails are set then this will reduce any damage. If the spinnaker is still set then you have a problem. Cut it free. The water load of a spinnaker will break most masts. It may be necessary to remove the rig.

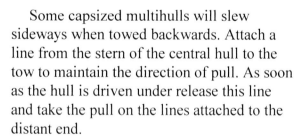

Some capsized multihulls will slew sideways when towed backwards. Attach a line from the stern of the central hull to the tow to maintain the direction of pull. As soon as the hull is driven under release this line and take the pull on the lines attached to the distant end.

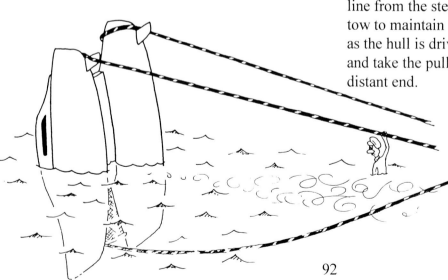

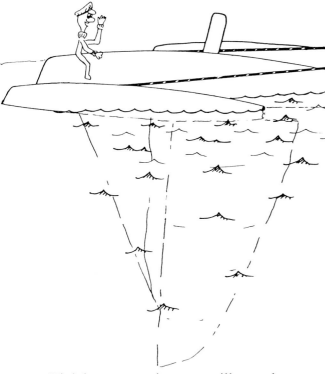

High buoyancy trimarans will tow along upside down and the stern will not drive under enough or create enough resistance to roll the yacht back upright.

This is because the rotational direction of the pull is less than the force needed to drive the sterns under. There are two options here. Either change the direction of the tow by elevating the take-off on the trimaran. This can be done by inserting two strongly mounted 'A' frames on the inverted hulls with 'V' tops so that the tow line can be run through this and then down to the bow. The bow pull is then at a higher take-off angle. The second option is to sink the sterns by flooding the floats. More than a hole in the inverted waterline will be needed. You may have to actually pump water into the stern of the floats. This can be done with a portable bilge pump, an ice pick and a nozzle. The hole can be temporarily filled with a wooden plug once righted.

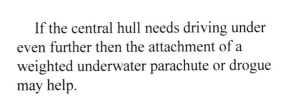

If the central hull needs driving under even further then the attachment of a weighted underwater parachute or drogue may help.

93

As you tow the inverted multihull along backwards, the water filled sterns and the drogue resisted central hull will drive under and the angle of pull will be such the that yacht will right end over end.

Capsized catamarans can utilise much of the same principles.

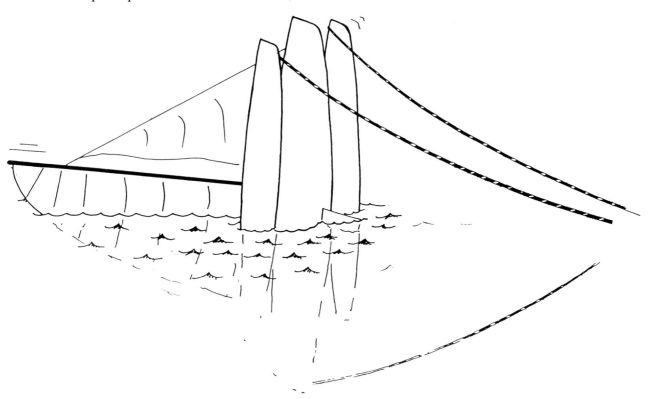

Towing upside down is an option if done slowly. The aim would be to get to a safe harbour where a crane can be utilised in righting the multihull. The rig may be damaged but this can be avoided by unbolting it and loading it aboard the tow boat.

Suggested equipment needed on the tow boat includes:
- Lots of strong line (enough for at least three tow lines)
- Large shifter, heavy duty rigging wire cutters
- Jury mast bars with lots of holes either end for rope lashings
- Portable bilge pump, ice pick, wooden through hull plugs
- Scuba gear.

94

ROLLER FURLING

Mainsail roller furling around the boom requires careful design. The battens should be parallel with the boom and the topping lift should support the boom at the right angle to stop the mainsail creeping forward onto the gooseneck and jamming. Ensure the outhaul is on tight. If your sail loses shape when it is furled then the slack section can be taken up by jamming clothing in the central bagged section of the boom. Reef points are needed for the storm sail reef loads.

Furling into the mast is rarely used on multihulls because it does not operate with battens.

If your multihull has running backstays then these should be used always to assist in developing forestay tension. Tightening the mainsheet will also tighten the forestay. Use all methods to tighten the forestay when furling. This reduces the wear on the furling gear. Trimarans have less problems with roller furling because of the rigidity of the central hull and increased forestay tension.

Multihulls do not heel with gusts so all sails should be of stronger manufacture than an equivalent one for a monohull.

A furling headsail makes a poor storm sail. The foot elevates and the central area of the sail is the fullest making a partially furled headsail inefficient when furled. Alternative systems include slab reefing the headsail onto the deck or having a separate storm jib that can be mounted on a cutter stay. In storm conditions the area of a furled headsail becomes significant windage.

BLOWN OUT II

Headsail furling is popular with cruising and shorthanded multihull sailors. There are some problems that need to be addressed.

On a catamaran the forestay tension is usually less that on yachts with central hulls. The joints in a furling system therefore work more. The less joints the less likely any problems.

Multihull Seamanship Rule:
Always carry a storm jib.

The ability to remove the headsail is important. In many storms a flogging, torn furling headsail spells disaster.

SAILS

Reefing

Reefing a multihull is similar to monohulls except when attempting to reef while running downwind. It is possible to be caught running downwind with too much sail up and be concerned about rounding up to reef. By working quickly the mainsail can sometimes be reefed without rounding up. Here is how it is done.

Tighten the luff downhaul as much as possible. Bear away quickly and have the main halyard ready to release. As soon as the apparent wind drops to near zero let the halyard go. The tension on the downhaul should bring the main flying down. To reach each reef point have the downhaul tension on the appropriate cunningham eye. When you set up the main halyard a useful hint is to have it running through two clutches so that one can be preset at the next reef height during this manoeuvre.

If you have to round up then lift the centreboards and bring the main in slightly on the traveller. As you start to round up release the mainsail so that it is feathering while beam on. Next time reef earlier.

Design and manufacture

Multihull sails should be made with the yacht speed and higher apparent wind strength in mind.

Multihull Seamanship Rule:
Have your multihull sails made by a sailmaker familiar with a multihulls different loads and sheeting angles.

On multihulls the sheeting angles are usually narrower. The premise that multihull sails should always be flat does not hold except for over-powered day sailing cats. A well reefed, well shaped mainsail and storm jib is much more efficient than a feathering, flat set of sails. Your multihull will also point to windward much better. The use of tight sheeting angles and efficient aerofoils is the key to efficient windward work when reefed.

BEAR AWAY!

SEAWEED & FISH NETS

Catching seaweed or a fishing line on the rudder is a potential disaster if steering is lost. Kick up rudders solve the problem quickly but only if the system of raising the rudders is readily set up. Consider where you will be sailing. If obstacles such as weed, lobster pots or fish traps are numerous then a lifting rudder may be an essential safety design requirement. Usually any debris creates enormous drag. There are a number of ways to remove the caught lines. The best system is to not have it catch in the first place. Mini-keels forward of the rudder may help. Alternatively a blade mounted under the hull and angled forward will cut any lines. Many offshore racing yachts use these to avoid having to slow down.

An alternative way of removing flotsam or jetsam is to cut it with a knife mounted on an extendible boathook.

Multihull Seamanship Rule:
Always carry a strong, extendible boathook.

Waterproof tape will usually suffice in securing the knife. If that fails then remember that you can sail a multihull backwards. That alone may be enough to disentangle the debris. To sail backwards round up into the wind and go into 'irons', sheet in the mainsail central on the traveller. Finally, if you have to go into the water always stop the yacht, down sails and wear a harness.

Debris also can be caught around propellers. Folding or collapsible propellers have a lower risk of catching lines but are still a potential problem. A keel forward of the propeller helps. A number of shaft 'cutting' fittings are available. These slice any wrapped line or weed from the shaft when the motor is started.

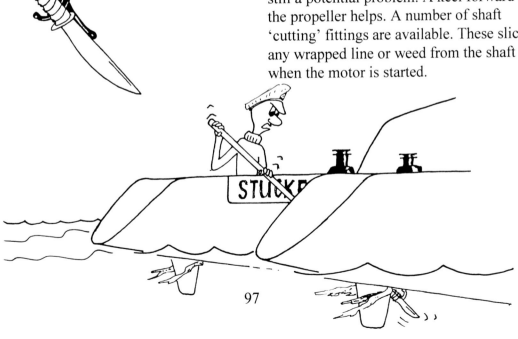

SELF STEERING & AUTOPILOTS

If your autopilot cannot handle the steering adjustment needed to maintain course then slow down and/or balance your yacht.

Multihulls cover ground quickly. By the time a kettle boils you could cover five nautical miles. A fast ship coming toward you could cover ten miles. That combination is the horizon on a clear day.

Multihull Seamanship Rule:
Keep a lookout.

Electronic autopilots have various 'extras' that assist fast sailing. Wind vane correction works on cruising multihulls but be wary of the effect of apparent wind. The apparent wind direction may not alter as your multihull accelerates into a reach. Off-course alarms are thus a good idea.

Electronic autopilots

Electronic autopilots work well on multihulls. The multiple long narrow hulls track well and the autopilot has less weight of vessel to turn. Intelligent autopilots can allow for the variation in direction that occurs as waves are sailed over. On multihulls with multiple rudders the steering ability of autopilots is further increased.

If your autopilot is exposed the high spray factor should be allowed for and the electronics protected as much as possible. Tiller mounted autopilots are usually stowed until needed. Storing a piece of electronic equipment in a damp, mouldy locker is not a good idea as your autopilot is not destined for a long life. Build a dry padded box to store your autopilot.

Multihull Seamanship Rule:
Look after your autopilot and it will look after you.

Wind vane steering

This works in light winds and on cruising multihulls with slower acceleration. The ability of a faster multihull to bend the apparent wind makes wind vane self steering unreliable. Setting up wind vane self steering is difficult on a catamaran and often requires a separate trim rudder mounted on a central pod. The central rudder on a trimaran is more suitable. The simplest system is a wind vane connected to a servo tab on an outboard skeg rudder. On certain points of sail these work well.

SHEET SYSTEMS

Multihulls have high loads on sheeting systems due to the inability to heel over and spill wind. For this reason multihulls should be reefed earlier and the sheets systems stronger. Ensure that your sheets are of appropriate strength and have no deterioration evident. If you use the 'replace when it breaks' philosophy then expect them to go in a gale, on a lee shore, while you are standing near the rope.

Multihull Seamanship Rule:
Always have a sharp solid knife available.

A knife may be the only way to release a trapped sheet. A good multihull sailor will have a large knife mounted in the cockpit and a sheathed one in their sailing clothes. A folding pocket knife is not an option in an emergency. The time and two hands needed to unfold one may be too much to avert disaster.

To cut kevlar or spectra sheets you may need a knife with a very sharp serrated section. Test your knife.

Sheet systems

The layout of sheets needs to be carefully thought through. Every turn, every block and every extra piece of hardware are potential snags for sheet lines. The ability to have sheets run free is one of the most important safety features of multihulls.

Use the K.I.S.S. principle when laying out sheet lines - whether they be headsail, mainsail or spinnaker sheets. Keep It Simple!

Determine the likely loads in advance and minimise the number of turns around winches and through blocks. Many large offshore racing multihulls have a simple two-to-one purchase on the mainsheet and a good strong winch and quick release cleat. Do not use lots of purchase blocks or an undersized winch that needs lots of turns to be effective. Quick release is not possible on these.

Tell new crewman never to stand over or on a loaded sheet. If accidentally released or if the line breaks they can be life threatening.

SINKING

Although they do not carry large quantities of ballast to drag them to the bottom within seconds of being holed, some multihulls will sink. If the construction material is positively buoyant then there is a higher chance that the fully flooded hulls will float. Aluminium hulls do not float. Solid fibreglass does not float.

Any multihull made from negatively buoyant material needs to have built in buoyancy compartments. All multihulls should have a collision bulkhead and enough separate, sealable compartments to ensure the flooded hull has enough buoyancy to stay afloat.

Bilge pump systems should be installed to enable all compartments to be pumped out after the hole is plugged. A high capacity portable bilge pump is an essential item.

Being positively buoyant does not mean you will always have something to remain aboard. Fire, destruction by collision or severe structural failure may all leave you in the water if you do not carry a liferaft. If you cannot swim ashore then you need another way of staying afloat!

There are a few occasions when you may want to partially sink or pump water into your multihull e.g. ballasting in a cyclone or while trying to right a multihull after capsize. If you decide to sink or flood a hull, then be aware of the damage that can occur by water surging up and down compartments. Bulkheads can be torn free and lead to major structural problems.

A flooded hull on a catamaran can cause the yacht to capsize as lateral stability is lost. The natural tendency is for the catamaran to turn side onto the waves when one hull is substantially heavier than the other. To avoid this capsize risk deploy a parachute to hold the bows toward the oncoming waves. This will also reduce the structural stress on the beams from surging water.

Trimarans with a flooded central hull can usually continue to sail although much slower. The capsize risk is less then if an outer hull is flooded.

SLIPPING

Multihull Seamanship Rule:
Prepare your slipping technique well in advance and allow double the estimated time.

Cradle or trailer slipping

Multihulls have advantages and disadvantages when being cradle or trailer slipped. The wide beam means removing cradle arms and adding supports for the hulls. The stability of having two or more hulls on a cradle means less problems with loads and rocking.

Slipped in a cyclone or gale

If you are unfortunate enough to be caught on the hard during extreme conditions then prepare. Your multihull needs to be secured down and protected. Drop the boat as low as possible to the earth. Ideally dig a hole and sit it in it! Attach chains from chainplates to steel stakes driven well into the ground. Weigh the hulls down by pumping water in the bilges and filling water tanks. If possible remove the mast.

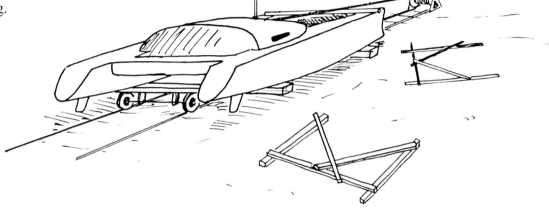

Multihulls without long keels need plenty of lengthwise support to spread the load evenly over the bottom of the hull. Try and locate the load points near the bulkheads.

Catamarans can be supported under the beams rather than the hulls but ensure that the pressure points can take the load. If in doubt use the hulls - they are designed to take the weight of the boat.

Because the vessel cannot orientate itself into the wind the mast may set up harmonics and vibrate dramatically - breaking ties, loading the stays and potentially damaging the hull where it is sitting on the ground.

A major source of damage on land will be flying debris. Boat yards are notorious for sheets of timber and metal lying around. Use the time before the cyclone to clean up and secure what you can.

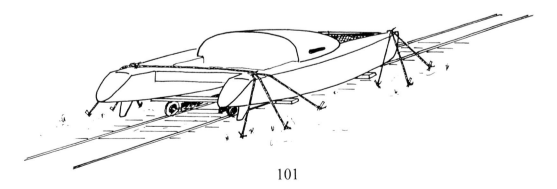

Sling slipping

It is uncommon to find a sling wide enough to cater for a multihull. Some narrower beam multihulls can be slung but beware of the bilateral compression loads on the beams.

Locate the slings around bulkheads and secure the multihull from heeling in the sling i.e. one hull being lifted first and rotating the boat.

On the hard

Once on the hard each hull needs support, especially if the mast has been removed and the yacht will be on the hard for some time. Most multihulls have some flexibility. If a catamaran is supported only under the beams both hulls may sag slightly. Similarly the floats on a trimaran may drop if only the main hull is supported. The significance of this will be obvious when you re-launch. The stays may not be long enough!

The more rigid multihulls such as full bridgedeck catamarans and trimarans still require support. Any structural work or built in additions - furniture, bulkheads, doorways or windows - need to be built with the boat in the launched trim. You may find doors will not close or minor load cracks appear.

Craning out

Know how your multihull balances when attempting to crane out. Because the crane needs to lean out further over the water, the ability of it to lift a weight is reduced. This is not normally a problem for lighter multihulls but needs consideration in heavier cruising types. If the mast remains up watch for it hitting the crane arm. Attachment points for the crane slings include under the main beams, around the hull(s) or onto chainplates (if strong enough).

SPINNAKERS

Light multihulls achieve high speeds downwind by running an asymmetrical spinnaker and flying it shy. By building up a high apparent wind (keeping the breeze that is felt either on or just forward of the beam) it is possible to carry the apparent wind direction forward. Very often the multihull will be heading well downwind (from the true wind) yet the apparent wind remains beam on.

The wide beam of multihulls enables traditional spinnakers to be set without a pole. By bracing the spinnaker with a line from each outboard bow and one from the middle hull (or beam) the spinnaker tack is variable in position.

A short spinnaker pole can be permanently mounted on the middle hull (or middle of a catamarans forward beam) to provide a rigid position for the tack. The advantage of this system is that there is only one line to tighten when setting the tack in most reaching positions.

It is still important to have the ability to pull the tack to windward. This is because in very light winds asymmetrical kites set from the mid-line will collapse or force you to sail way off course with a resultant poor velocity made good (VMG) downwind.

On high performance multihulls it is possible to keep the headsail up when running under spinnaker. On racing yachts there is a definite advantage to trimming and maintaining as much sail area as possible - the mainsail, the headsail and the spinnaker. To achieve this the sails should have efficiently mounted telltales and the crew should be aware of the need to work the sheets to maintain your multihull 'in the groove'. The aim is to keep the apparent wind moving across the boat at about 90 degrees. (See the chapter on Telltales.)

Gybing a spinnaker with a permanent tack position requires two long sheet lines. These are run either inside or outside the halyard depending on wind strength.

In very light conditions run the lines inside so when the kite collapses the clew can be pulled through manually to the other side. In every other wind level run the lines outside. The gybe technique is to 'blow' the sheet so the sail is blown outboard as the multihull goes through the gybe. When the wind changes quarters the new sheet can be hauled in. Ensure all lines are free to run unobstructed.

Multihull Seamanship Rule:
When under spinnaker be aware of the
downwind true wind strength.

A kite that will carry 20 knots of apparent wind might still be up when the true wind exceeds 30 knots. Not a good idea.

Spinnaker wrap

This problem occurs when the spinnaker collapses due to surfing (when the apparent wind goes to zero) or bearing away too much (spinnaker blanketed behind the mainsail). The central part of the spinnaker folds back onto the forestay and wraps around it, locking itself. The rest of the spinnaker is caught in a circular wind and then wraps around the forestay. No amount of pulling or releasing sheets, track or halyard will release it.

The solution is to gybe the mainsail and sail off on the other downwind tack. The rotating wind in front of the mainsail is reversed in direction and the spinnaker will unwrap by itself. The sheets will be set wrong when it does release so be prepared to gybe the mainsail as soon as the spinnaker has unwound.

Spinnaker wraps can be avoided by hoisting a net sail on the forestay or by leaving the jib set. Careful sheet trimming and good helmsman concentration will also reduce the risk of a wrap.

STEERING & RUDDERS

Multihull rudders have to have enough area to operate at low speeds but be small enough not to create excessive drag at high speeds.

Specific problems occur when a rudder loses its grip on the water at high speeds. Control from the helm is lost until either the multihull slows or the rudder is turned hard and steering returns. This cavitation or ventilation results when air is sucked down the low pressure side of the blade.

A trimaran, having one rudder in most cases, is out of control if the rudder ventilates. Transom hung rudders are more prone to ventilation, especially if the yacht or rudder is not well balanced. Transom hung rudders perform poorly in steep following seas due to the decrease in the amount of the foil in the water. Shallow rudders are similarly less effective in these conditions. Loss of steerage in these conditions is one component involved in diagonal capsize.

The more lee or weather helm correction needed the greater the pressure difference on either side of the rudder and thus the more likely air will be sucked down and cause ventilation. Ventilation plates, running parallel with the water line, will reduce this likelihood although balancing the yacht and rudder would be a better idea.

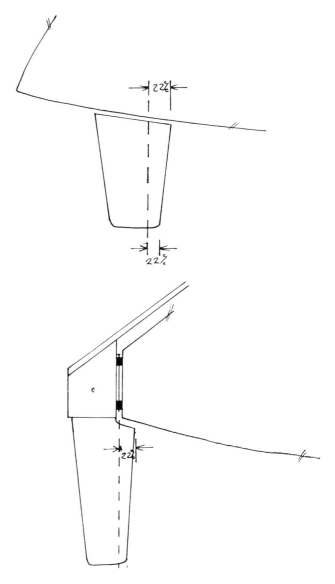

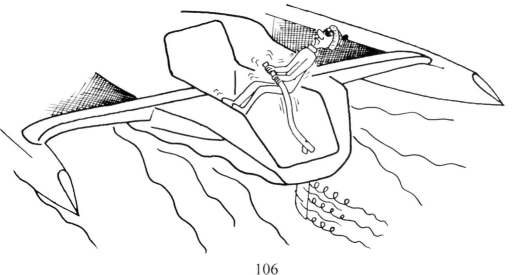

A light responsive helm requires the rudder to be balanced about the pivot axis. The effective centre of pressure for a hydrofoil of symmetrical section is about 25% aft of the leading edge for cruising multihulls and 13% aft of the leading edge for racing multihulls.

Once ventilation has occurred it is useless to continue to push the helm in the same direction. Flow may be restored by rapidly alternating the helm direction forcefully over a few seconds. On trimarans, loss of steering may also be the result of turbulent flow generated from the centreboard. At high speeds the centreboard should be up as high as possible to avoid this.

Jury rudders and steering

A traditional jury steering system is difficult to make if you do not have the classic long, movable spinnaker pole. There is a better way for multihulls. The wide beam on a multihull can be utilised to steer the boat by running a drogue astern mounted on a bridle.

Multihull Seamanship Rule:
Practice and perfect your jury rudder system.
Use the beam advantage.

By adjusting the bridle arms the relative pressure on each hull varies and thus steers the yacht. This works in all but very light conditions when you will need to motor to generate resistance on the drogue. See the illustration in the Bridles chapter.

STORM SAILING

Heavy weather management

The way you manage storm conditions depends on:
• Knowledge of your multihulls characteristics in heavy weather
• Proximity of shelter
• Direction you wish to sail
• Dangers - lee shore, reefs, shipping routes.

Tactical alternatives

The following tactics will be discussed in detail:
• Windward storm sailing
    Use of the storm jib
    Use of the storm mainsail
• Downwind storm sailing
    Sailing tactics downwind
    Running warps and drogues
• Stopping
    Parachute sea anchors
    Lying ahull
    Heaving to
• Special considerations
    Wing masts.

Avoiding storms

The speed of a multihull can be used to avoid weather patterns by either heading for port or sailing to the area where the least effect will be felt. In reality this requires accurate, regular weather forecasting and good routing skills.

In cyclonic conditions your yacht can be directed to the safe quarter as follows:

In the Southern Hemisphere, with your back to the wind, the safe quarter is on your left. Broad reaching in this direction will put you away from the lowest pressure area.

In the Northern Hemisphere, with your back to the wind, the safe quarter is on your right. Broad reaching in this direction will put you away from the lowest pressure area.

Deck preparation for a storm

When a storm is approaching and it has to be confronted at sea then the deck can be set up to make life safer and easier. Your multihull will be confronting high winds and waves that will break across the decks. You may need to tow drogues or set a parachute sea anchor. Storm headsails, storm reefed mainsails or bare poles may be needed as survival tactics. The following can be done to prepare for the worst:
• Double lash every object that has to remain on deck e.g. dinghy, sailboard, spare fuel tanks etc.
• Remove all unnecessary lines. Stow them for easy and quick access below deck.
• Prepare the parachute sea anchor and the drogue lines in a neat pile. Have the parachute and drogue ready for deployment. Stow the equipment so that it is not washed overboard or tangled if the cockpit is pooped (filled by a wave).
• Have the helm area protected and give the helmsman access to essential equipment - a white signalling flare should ships approach too close, access to plenty of snacks and drinks, binoculars and torch.

Windward storm sailing

As a survival tactic sailing to windward on a multihull has some advantages. You remain in control. The bows of the multihull have momentum to punch through waves. The worst breakers can be avoided or approached at the optimum angle.

On the negative side it is hard to stay alert in stressful conditions. There are times when you will need to keep sailing. Clawing off a lee shore or sailing away from a weather pattern are two examples.

To point effectively in high wind conditions your well reefed sails should have narrow sheeting angles and some shape. Flat blades widely sheeted do not point.

Sails should be adjusted as wind strength increases. Move the sheeting points to leeward and allow the sails to twist. This is achieved by sheeting the jib further out and back and by sheeting the main down the traveller and eased slightly.

Motor sailing with diesel engines and a storm jib is a very effective way of clawing to windward in storm conditions.

Sailing a multihull to windward can be very uncomfortable. The motion is quick, jerking and the hulls may leap off the back of waves. The solution to this is simple.

Multihull Seamanship Rule:
If you are uncomfortable sailing to windward slow down.

It sounds easy and it is. To slow down you can either reduce sail or tow a drogue. Towing a drogue evens the speed out and works well on occasions. The aim is to keep driving forward and to roll rather than leap over waves.

The higher speed of a multihull develops a higher apparent wind when windward sailing. Exposure, and thus fatigue, is a real risk. At the best you could have an enclosed helm. At the worst you should have a fully enclosed helmet to add to your wet weather gear.

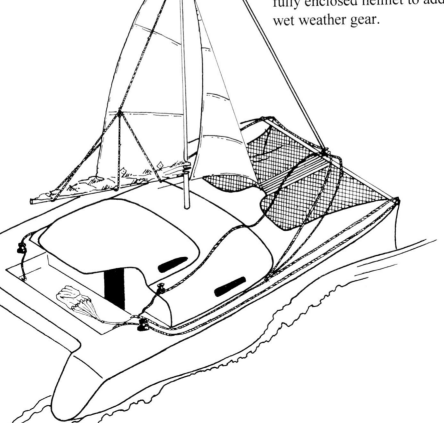

Multihull Seamanship Rule:
Always be prepared for wet windward sailing.

An ideal solution to exposure is the use of surfing helmets. These are lightweight, have full ultraviolet ray protecting face shields and enough ventilation to wear for days. Canopies, dodgers and spray shields should all be tested before you need them.

Most wharfs have a fire hose. Ask and borrow a few minutes of blasting water to see if your protection will hold up when it matters.

The fatigue factor on beams and rig increases enormously when pounding to windward. Dropping off the back of a wave face often gives false readings on masthead wind instruments. This 'flicking effect' results in stories of 70 knot winds when the reality might be half that and steep wave action. Never the less the wind experienced at the masthead whilst driving into a sea is a stronger apparent wind and your equipment and rig must be designed and prepared for it.

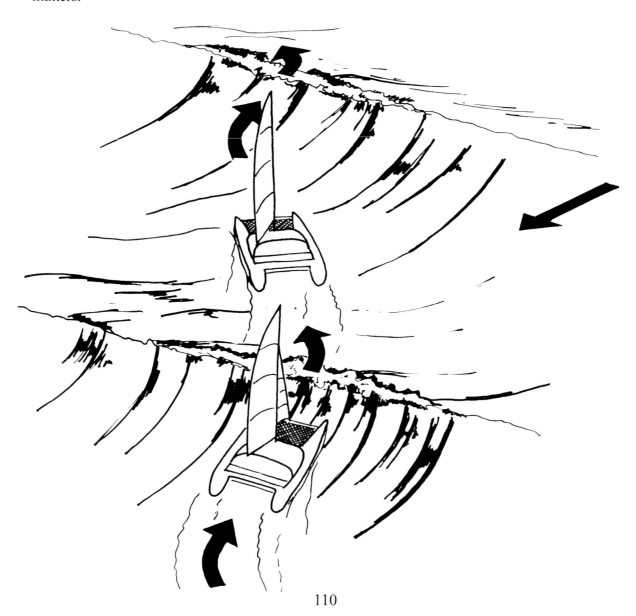

110

Sailing to windward into big, steep waves requires careful helm work. You need to bear away sharply at the top of these waves to prevent falling off the peaks. Sailing to windward is wetter and windier than any other direction.

Tacking and stalling

Multihull Seamanship Rule:
If you think you will stall during a tack in storm conditions then consider a controlled gybe.

In a rough sea with minimal sail and centreboards partially raised tacking can be difficult and dangerous. The danger is stalling part way through the tack and falling backwards on a wave. If the rudders are not held firmly they can spin sideways and potentially break. Capsize is possible if the multihull slides side onto the waves without forward motion. Having to back the jib and reverse around is dangerous. If in doubt run with the sea and gybe to get onto the new tack. You will lose some windward ground but the risks are less. Do not perform any tack or gybe with too much sail up.

The storm jib

No multihull should leave the mooring without a storm jib. These are life savers. The windward performance of a multihull is dependent on a balanced rig. You will need one to crawl off a lee shore in a gale. A multihull sailing under storm jib and trimmed rotating mast will even sail to windward. To run downwind under warps or drogue a storm jib will keep the bows downwind.

Roller furling headsails do not work as storm sails. This is because the foot climbs upward as most headsails are furled. Sail area up high is not what you need in a gale. When half rolled the shape is distorted so much that all it develops is drag and no drive. Multihulls with roller furling headsails should have a cutter rig arrangement (it need not be a permanent cutter stay) to enable the storm jib to be hanked on inside the fully furled headsail. Before a storm remove the headsail completely off the furler.

The storm mainsail

A storm trysail is rarely seen on multihulls. A storm is not the time to be hanking on a new sail. The more practical alternative is to have an equally strong fourth 'storm' reef section in the mainsail. This section of the sail needs to be heavily reinforced at both the tack, clew and along the reefed foot.

To qualify under Category 'O' offshore safety standards the smallest mainsail reef must be less then 15% of the mainsail area. To make this area of sail work it is important that the reefed sail lying in the lazyjacks is firmly stowed. A line of reef eyelets is essential. The cunningham eye section at the front of the storm reef needs to be secured in two directions - around the mast and toward the deck. If necessary lash it with stout line.

Downwind storm sailing

Downwind sailing can be an exhilarating ride. Racing multihulls can surf regularly at over 25 knots. Most cruising multihulls are at risk of broaching or losing rudder control at speeds over 20 knots.

Wave fronts travel at varying speeds. A three metre wave may travel at 20 knots. Large storm waves at up to 40 knots.

Running downwind as a storm survival tactic requires understanding of the weather. Most areas have a typical storm track. Being aware of these and the changes in wind direction will enable an assessment to be made of where you should head for. It is essential that an accurate log is kept of wind direction to determine your tactics. Plot the storm front on a chart.

Multihull Seamanship Rule:
Know your position relative to the storm centre before deciding course changes.

Downwind storm sailing needs sea room and lots of it. Under drogue and warps your multihull may still average five to ten knots - 240 miles a day. Without a drogue a multihull will start surfing as the wind and waves build. By reducing sail the tendency to surf will be reduced but eventually most multihulls will surf under bare poles in storm conditions.

Multihull Seamanship Rule:
When sailing downwind note the true wind speed every few minutes.

Because of the high boat speed of a multihull the true wind can be deceptively strong. For example, your multihull may be able to carry two reefs and a working jib in 20 knots of apparent wind while sailing downwind at 15 knots boat speed. The problem will occur when you have to round up to reef in 35 knots of true wind!

Multihull Seamanship Rule:
Carry the amount of sail for the true wind, not the apparent wind. Reef to the gusts.

One experience of rounding up overpowered in gale conditions is one experience too many.

Multihull Seamanship Rule:
When trailing warps or drogues bridle them for directional stability.

Capsize occurs commonly when broached or hit by a rogue wave from a different direction. A bridled drogue will slow any tendency to turn your multihull sideways to a wave face.

Despite the best preparation any vessel can be overwhelmed by a huge breaking wave.

Try not to sail directly down waves or at right angles to their direction. It is best to sail down the face at a slight angle with control. If you have to sail straight down the face always tow an efficient drogue.

Drogues and warps in a storm

A line and chain warp towed astern will slow your multihull in moderate conditions. To increase the resistance objects can be added to the line - these are called drogues.

Multihull Seamanship Rule:
Always have your drogue and bridle ready for deployment.

A drogue is a friction device towed behind a multihull sailing downwind. They can be used to reduce overall speed, stop or slow surfing down waves, reduce broaching tendencies by stabilising direction and ease loads on the rudders and helm. A bridle mounted drogue can even be used as emergency steering. Sailing downwind under storm sails alone is not enough to stop pitch-poling or broaching. This is especially true in gusty conditions with steep seas. Use a drogue.

Multihull Seamanship Rule:
When running downwind with a drogue raise your centreboards.

Centreboards raised moves the centre of lateral resistance toward the stern and reduces side to side swinging (yawing).

Available drogues

In an emergency ground anchors have been used by towing them astern. These twist, spin and roll and dramatic knots may occur in the rode or chain. A CQR anchor works reasonably well if towed backwards. Anchor chain can also be towed alone and the drag can be increased by tying it into a big knot. No matter which anchor is used the multihull will be slowed.

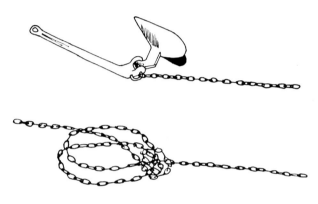

A car tyre drogue is often stated as a cheap drogue. These work until you really need them - at high speeds they sit on the water surface and skid. A much better idea is to set up a drogue specifically designed for the purpose. There are a number of proprietary drogues available. These range from moulded plastic or metal devices through to cloth cones and small parachute shapes.

Larger multihulls require a substantial device to handle the high loads needed to slow them down. The proprietary drogues come in different sizes designed for these loads. The metal conical drogues have specialised slots which open at a pre-adjusted setting. These slots increase the turbulence and thus slow the boatspeed.

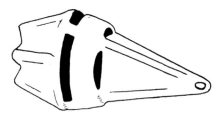

The smaller, plastic conical drogues have fixed slots that work continuously. These are generally suitable for multihulls up to 12 metres in length.

The drawback of the metal or plastic conical drogues all take up valuable storage space.

A compact, light weight drag device is a material or webbing drogue. These can be like miniature parachutes or cone shaped. Water is caught in the wide end of the cone and exits the narrow end. The partially trapped water is dragged along. As the water exits it creates further turbulence to retard forward movement. The advantage of a material drogue is that it is stowed in a small bag and can be permanently stored in a cockpit locker or hung in a transom bag.

Drogue set-up

The drogue tether or rode should be able to stretch. Braded nylon is best. Stranded nylon has the tendency to unravel under heavy loads. Dacron or polyester lines have reduced elasticity and thus a longer rode length is required if these are used. Rode diameter should be equivalent to the normal anchor rode (which is ideal).

All drogues are useless stored away and untested. The line set up is critical to their working properly.

A bridle should be used to achieve maximum directional stability. If a bridle is used then it needs to be tested so the tether length is easily adjusted. The bridle should be between 1.5 and 2.5 times the multihull beam. Bridle arms too short do not work.

If the lines are too long they will probably twist. This is not a major problem as the twist should stop and leave enough length in the bridle arms for them to remain effective. The problem is untangling the twist when adjustment is needed.

The ideal bridle would be a permanently rigged setup that can be tied to the rode with a rolling hitch. Let the rode weight be taken by the bridle but secure the rode left inside the 'y' without tension as a backup.

Steering is possible both by using the helm and by adjusting the bridle arm lengths. Some centreboard down may be needed.

The tether length is critical to drogue operation. If the drogue is in the face of the following wave when your multihull starts to surf, then it may leap out of the wave and surf down in parallel with your multihull.

Conical metal and plastic drogues sometimes 'porpoise' and need a short length of chain attached to them to reduce this tendency.

The drogue tether should be adjusted regularly to be a half wave length out of sync with your boat i.e. at least 1 1/2 waves behind when you are on the peak of a wave. When your multihull starts to surf the drogue has to be pulled through the following wave, retarding the acceleration.

Wave and sea states change with tide, sea bottom and wind conditions. For effective use of a drag device the tether must be adjustable and the length reviewed regularly.

Multihull Seamanship Rule:
Drogue tethers need regular length adjustment - do not wait for the drogue to stop working.

As waves build in height they increase in length.

You can run more than one drogue. In emergency situations, where you have to run downwind and need as much drag and directional stability as possible, many lines can be run astern. Do not forget available lines such as halyards etc. To help rethread your mast halyards have a fine line available to run as a feeder 'mouse' through the blocks. A 'mouse' is a 3-5 mm diameter line that can be taped or spliced onto the end of the line you wish to remove and run along its course as the halyard is removed. It will be there when you need to put the halyard back.

Multihull Seamanship Rule:
Know what a halyard mouse is and use one to access extra rode lines.

Sheet and halyard lines have minimal stretch and elasticity so do not use them exclusively as either drogue or sea anchor rodes.

Swivels do not stop rode twists or stranded ropes from unravelling. Under load they simply do not work except to add some weight to the line. Beware of stainless steel swivels which can have undetectable fatigue problems due to salt crystal corrosion. Sudden failure of stainless steel components has led to the loss of some drogue and sea anchor set-ups.

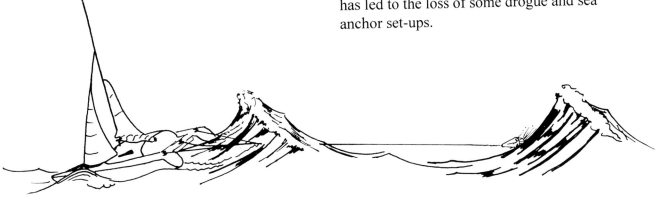

Stopping

There are three recognised techniques for stopping at sea:
• Parachute sea anchoring
• Lying a-hull
• Heaving-to.

It is possible to anchor at sea - not to the sea bed but to the ocean itself. Your multihull is then moving only at the rate of the water currents. Parachute sea anchoring is the ultimate survival technique when the crew is exhausted, the conditions disastrous and your multihull at risk of capsize. It can also be a way of 'parking at sea', a useful skill when awaiting tides or daylight to enter ports or to stop downwind drift if the boat is crippled by damage or cannot sail off a lee shore.

Parachute sea anchors

Parachute sea anchor manufacturers have recommended size parachutes for the displacement weight of each multihull. The size is important because if the parachute is too small the bows will blow off and put the vessel beam on the approaching waves.

If your parachute sea anchor does not hold the bows into the wind then do not set it off the bow. It can be set off the stern as a drogue but should be replaced with a bigger unit.

Parachute sea anchors should be set from the bow of the multihull on a nylon line (the 'rode' or 'tether') which is secured to the boat. A bridle should be attached to the rode and run through the blocks on the outboard bows. The free ends of the bridle lines must be secured to strong cleats. Keep the arrangement simple.(See chapter on Bridles).

The rode should be able to stretch therefore nylon is preferred over polyester or dacron.

The rope diameter should be equal to the multihulls normal anchor line (which is ideal). The minimum recommended rode length is 20 times the expected height of the waves. The use of a weight or some chain, located mid scope, provides catenary/ mechanical shock absorption. This can be added after deployment if needed by feeding it down on a snatch block.

A sea anchor parachute needs a small float attached to a line tied to the discharge outlet (the small opening in the top of the parachute). This stops the parachute from sinking too far under and pulling the bows down. Trip lines are not used on most multihulls because they cause foul ups. It is best to have the main tether line on a strong winch so that it can be winched home when the weather moderates.

When preparing for heavy weather the bagged parachute can be stored in the cockpit with the lines attached and ready. Similarly the bridle arrangement should be pre-set. The parachute is now able to be set without having to untangle and run lines in an emergency.

If extreme conditions are expected prepare early. If deemed necessary remove the mainsail and lash it below deck.

If your multihull has a roller furling headsail then remove the sail and set up the storm jib arrangement.

Launching the parachute sea anchor

Wet the parachute to help it sink and stick to the water. The safest launching technique involves rounding up into the wind (either under sail or motoring). Immediately drop all sail, secure the rudder amidships (straight), and as the multihull drifts off to one side deploy the parachute over the windward bow - never the leeward side. Control the rode run with a turn around a winch. As it runs give enough tension to fill the parachute and turn the bows into the wind. Secure the rode firmly and set your bridle lines. Check all chafe points. When finished check all chafe points again!

Centreboards should be lowered to reduce side to side drifting motion ('yawing'). Raise rudders if possible or lock in position amidships. This keeps the centre of lateral resistance forward.

Multihull Seamanship Rule:
All centreboards should be lowered when using a parachute sea anchor off the bow.

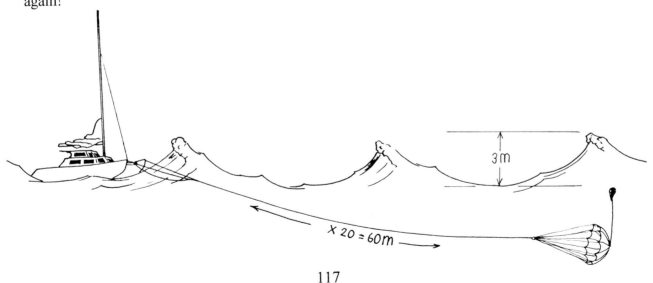

3m

X 20 = 60m

Parachute sea anchor problems

If your multihull is being yanked off wave tops and driven through waves, pulling deck hardware and possibly the parachute to bits then your rode needs to be longer and deeper. Add an anchor to the line as a catenary and lengthen the rode to reduce peak loads in the line.

Strand rope may untwist under load. This rotation might twist the shroud lines up and reduce the effective diameter of the parachute. Braided nylon is better. Swivels rarely help as they do not swivel under load.

Parachute sea anchor retrieval

Wait for calmer weather. Trip lines are a potential cause of tangles and are not recommended. Simply motor up to the parachute while winching or hauling the rode. The parachute will not break its shape until one of the shroud lines are reached. Haul these and the chute will collapse.

Parachute sea anchor care

Salt water crystals drying in the parachute material will weaken the material over time. Keep the parachute wet until it can be rinsed thoroughly in fresh water, dried and re-bagged. Storing the parachute in sealed garbage bags is one suggestion.

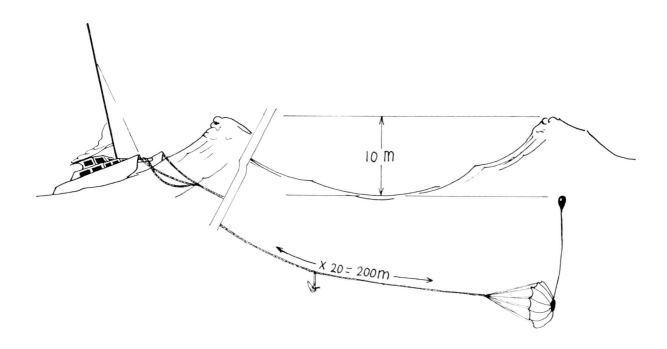

10 m

X 20 = 200m

Lying ahull

Lying ahull is dropping all sails and drifting under bare poles at the whim of the wind and waves. Waves break over the side hulls with tremendous impact and a multihulls wide beam will pound waves underneath.

High loads are put on beam structures when left to the ravages of the waves. Small multihulls can be tripped and flipped over. Lying ahull in storm conditions is a tactic only for the larger multihull.

A multihull lying ahull will drift downwind at speeds of up to five knots. Lightweight multihulls with the centreboards raised often turn slightly downwind as the centre of lateral resistance is moved aft and the hulls 'sail'. In moderate conditions this is fairly comfortable. In storm conditions it is not.

Heaving-to

Heaving-to means having the helm turned so the multihull is trying to round up into the wind but the headsail is 'aback'(sheeted on the wrong side) and the mainsail set normally. Depending on the hull shape, lateral resistance of keels and multihull length the resultant motion will vary from sailing too slowly forward to drifting on a broad reach. In moderate conditions it is a good way to pull up and rest or perform tasks such as a repair.

Multihull Seamanship Rule:
Trial your multihull lying ahull and heaved-to.

Only by testing will you know how your multihull will respond.

A global positioning satellite (GPS) navigator is invaluable when hove-to. It will give details of drift and current position whereas dead-reckoning is considerably inaccurate.

Wing masts in a storm

It is virtually impossible to feather a wing mast so it will not create drive. Without sails the mast will control the yacht, often taking the multihull in different directions to the rudder and/or drogues.

Multihull Seamanship Rule:
If sailing under a wing mast alone then the wing mast rules.

To balance the boat often a very tiny storm jib is needed. It will not make you go much faster but it will stop the wing mast from taking control.

Lying under a sea anchor with a wing mast is not much fun. It knocks the deck gear around and pushes waves over the boat as the multihull sails on the sea anchor. Only use a sea anchor on a multihull with a wing mast as a last resort.

Pin or lock the wing mast fore and aft when on a mooring in a storm. It then behaves like a normal mast and does not tend to drive the boat forward excessively. Never let the wing mast rotation control go loose in high winds as violent oscillations can develop and regaining control could easily cause injuries.

Multihull Seamanship Rule:
Always lock the mast rotation control in both directions.

This counters sea induced inertia forces and will stop oscillations developing.

STRESS MEASUREMENT & BEAM FAILURE

If you do not know the stresses that your multihull has endured how can you find out if the beams and rig are okay? The answer is via non-destructive testing. These are inspection services that have portable x-ray testing equipment specifically for metals. Aluminium masts and beams can be x-rayed or ultrasound tested for stress fractures that are invisible to the naked eye. The services are inexpensive and a great investment in your security offshore.

Before spending thousands on a second-hand multihull consider non-destructive testing as part of your pre-purchase survey.

Multihull Seamanship Rule:
Do not under estimate the stresses after any collision, extreme sailing conditions or prolonged use. Beams are highly loaded and need thorough inspection.

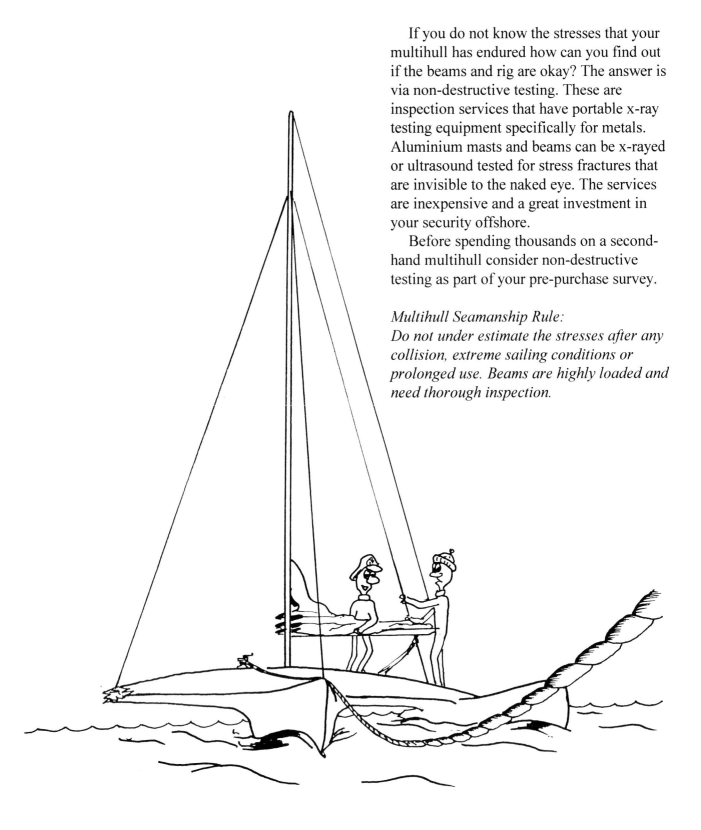

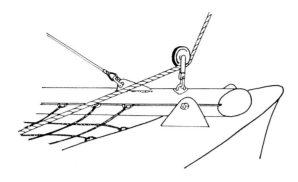

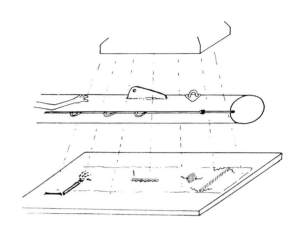

The mast and rig of a multihull are under greater stress loads than a monohull. A monohull heels to spill wind. A multihull converts the majority of the force into power.

After extended work your mast should be thoroughly inspected. A rigger will detect obvious faults. Areas of high stress can be specially painted to detect external fractures. Non-destructive testing can be carried out in most boat yards to detect internal fractures.

On aluminium tube beams check particularly around holes, through bolts and fittings. It is these stress concentration areas where cracks begin.

Beam failure

Should beam failure occur it need not be the end. The boom can be used as a splint to strengthen a partially fractured cross beam.

If a trimaran loses a float stability may be maintained. Drop sails and secure the mast by running any spare halyards to blocks or cleats on the damaged side. Swing the boom over to above the surviving float and if needed add ballast to the float (fuel containers, spare anchors etc.) Trimarans have been successfully towed for hundreds of miles like this.

TACKING & GYBING

A multihull is able to be easily tacked and gybed if it sails well to windward, does not have deep V hulls and has efficient rudders.

Tacking

The technique involves starting by sailing close to the wind with enough speed. Choose your moment where the wind is constant and there are no waves to rock the boat to a stop.

Push the helm gently and ease the jib sheet to start tacking. Excessive rudder angle may stall the boat.

As you bear away onto the new tack increase the rudder angle and ease the mainsheet slightly to accelerate the boat. If the boat goes about easily do not keep the jib aback. Sheet the jib over as fast as possible to help bearing away and get speed back.

Trim the jib correctly, sail at the optimum angle and re-trim the mainsail.

When tacking frequently (such as when working into a harbour) it may be difficult to tune the mainsail. In these instances it is better to trim the sail with more twist than usual to help gain speed on the new tack. If the wind is strong use a small headsail with minimal overlap.

Gybing

Gybing is made simple by the lack of broaching, increased boat speed (and thus reduced apparent wind) and a long mainsheet track to control the mainsail.

The technique involves steering the boat downwind while taking the slack out of the mainsheet.

Pull the traveller amidships i.e. into the centre.

Bear away to gybe the mainsail, controlling the traveller. Be wary as the powerful sail can move violently in a breeze or if you slow down too much.

Gybe the headsail when on the new bearing and re-trim the mainsail.

TARGA BAR & DAVITS

The targa bar is an inverted 'U' shaped beam that is raised off the back beam of a catamaran or aft section of a trimaran. 'Davits' are crane like arms with lifting slings or winch systems on their outer end for raising equipment aboard.

A targa bar is the ideal place on a multihull to mount solar panels. Here the panels will not interfere with deck operations and thus receive a higher percentage of sunlight.

The aft deck area of a multihull is often the place where other items tend to congregate - dinghy, liferaft, barbeques and fishing or diving gear. A lifting tackle can be incorporated into the targa bar and this can be used for raising the dinghy, securing it to the aft beam when raised. Be wary of carrying your dinghy on davits or the targa bar in rough seas. If the dinghy is pooped (filled) by a large wave from astern then the excessive weight may destroy the dinghy, davit or supports. To avoid this problem stow the dinghy upside down on deck, cover it with a tent shaped tarpaulin or tilt it sideways or upside down on the davit.

Any block and tackle or winch on the stern can be a useful hoist position for heavy objects, including a man overboard.

Be wary of adding a targa bar or davits to the stern of a multihull that was not designed with one originally. The weight factor, hanging over the stern, will affect the buoyancy distribution of the hulls and may seriously change the yachts trim.

On some designs the targa bar is used to carry the mainsheet track. This removes much of the clutter from the cockpit. The drawback is that it puts the sheets and blocks away from the view and quick access of the helmsman. It is essential that a quick dumping system be incorporated near the helmsman.

A targa bar creates windage. It should be as aerofoil and as light as possible within the strength range.

Other uses for a targa bar include sighting of the VHF, GPS, television and radio antennae. A deck light mounted underneath usually lights the cockpit and water off the stern well. Canopy attachment points on the front can provide dodger supports and extra hand holds may aid climbing on and off the sterns.

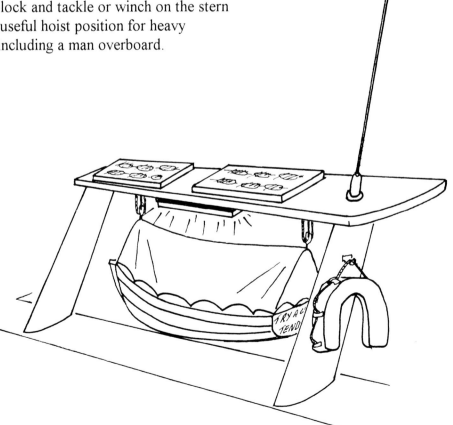

TELLTALES

Telltales are essential on any yacht and are more so on a multihull with its higher range of boat speed and apparent wind.

Multihull Seamanship Rule:
Multihull sails need telltales.

The following is a guide:
Each sail should have two sets of telltales. Each has a separate roll in determining trim.
On the mainsail of a multihull with a rotating mast fit the telltales about 20-25 cm (9"-12") from the luff (front of the sail). For a fixed mast double the distance back to 40-50 cm. The upper telltales should be mounted just above the hounds on a fractional rig or one third of the way from the top of the mast on a masthead rig. These telltales indicate how much you should sheet in the main. The lower telltales, positioned about a third of a way up the mainsail, indicate the position of the mainsail traveller.
On the headsail (or jib) set the telltales about 20-25 cm (9"-12") from the luff (front of the sail). The lower set one third up from the bottom of the sail, the upper set two thirds of the way up from the bottom of the sail.
On an asymmetrical spinnaker the telltales should be set 20-25 cm (9"-12") back from the luff (front of the sail). The same position can be used with a symmetrical spinnaker if one edge is used constantly as the leading edge. If not you will need four sets - two on each edge.

The upper telltales should be near the point that the spinnaker shape starts to curve sharply (known as the shoulder). The lower telltales should be positioned about 1/4 of the way up the sail.

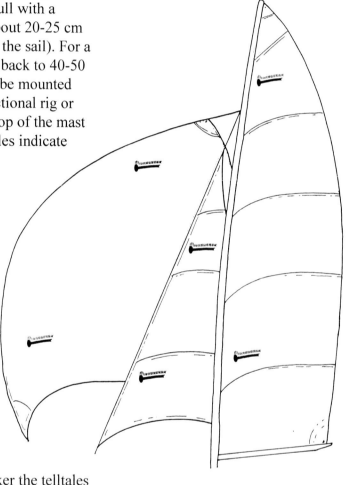

124

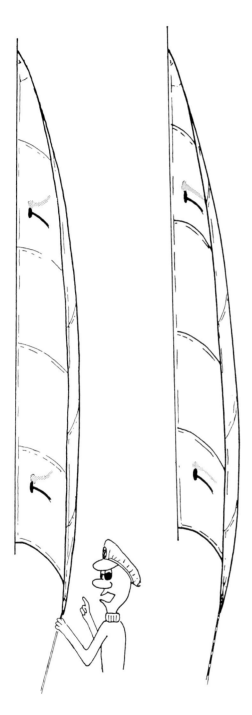

How to use a multihulls telltales

When running downwind set the spinnaker first. Have the front (the tack) mid line and sail so the wind is 90 degrees off the boat. Use the masthead wind indicator to maintain the multihull with the wind coming from the beam. Sheet the spinnaker in until it starts to stall. The telltales on the leeward (downwind) side of the sail will collapse and backwind at this point. Ease the spinnaker out until these are flying.

Next set the main. Bring the traveller in until the lower set of mainsail telltales start to stall. Then ease the main out slightly until they flow again. Now tighten the mainsheet. When the upper mainsail telltales start to stall ease the main slightly. It is now trimmed.

Finally sheet the jib in until it luffs slightly. The telltales on the leeward side will stall first. When this occurs ease the sheet slightly. All telltales should now be streaming nicely and your multihull will be charging along at maximum speed.

Multihull Seamanship Rule:
Set the spinnaker, then the main then the jib.
Sheet in until the leeward telltales stall and then out until they flow again.

Telltale settings for pointing upwind and reaching work in a similar fashion. On the main set the traveller into the position for optimum pointing ability then tighten the sheet to set the upper telltale. The telltales work more as a guide for the helmsman when working to windward - when they start to stall the helmsman is laying off or pointing too high. Most multihulls have optimum sail positions when pointing, varying for different wind strengths.

TOWING

The occasions when a multihull may require a tow are numerous. Examples include broken rudders, dismasting, motor failure, float damage or structural failure. Towing a multihull is best done with a bridle except for the occasion where a trimaran has lost a float. In this case it may be better to run only one line off the central hull.

The rescue vessel can pick up the float of a parachute streamed ahead and pull the rode aboard to secure the tow. This saves approaching the stricken multihull.

Towing downwind will be assisted by the multihull itself dragging a bridle set drogue. This will stop the multihull surfing and catching up to the tow boat. It will also keep an even strain on the tow line and reduce surging.

Tow attachment points on the multihull need to be strong enough to take the loads. On a catamaran the snatch block attachments for the spinnaker lines on the bows usually suffice. Many trimarans have similar although some racing trimarans do not.

Use the strongest outboard points e.g. beam attachments. Do not run a line off the mast - it is not designed to handle large lateral loads at the base.

Any water in the multihull will greatly slow the tow and thus should be pumped clear if possible.

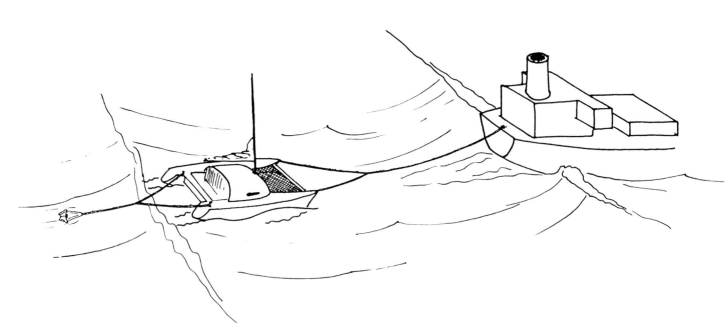

If you are to be towed by a ship at speed then distribute the weight in the multihull to facilitate stability i.e. low and central. This will reduce the risk of the bow riding under and stern being pooped by either the multihulls or the ships transverse wave formation.

Be wary of using a nylon anchor line as a tow rope - it has very large amounts of stored energy and can whip back and kill if it breaks. When towing make sure you are in step with the towing vessel i.e. you are both going up the face of a wave at the same time or down the face of a wave at the same time. This way you will avoid being pulled into the next wave or surfing up and hitting the tow vessel. Continue to monitor the tow closely and adjust the tow line as required. It does not matter how many waves are between the vessels - as long as they are in step.

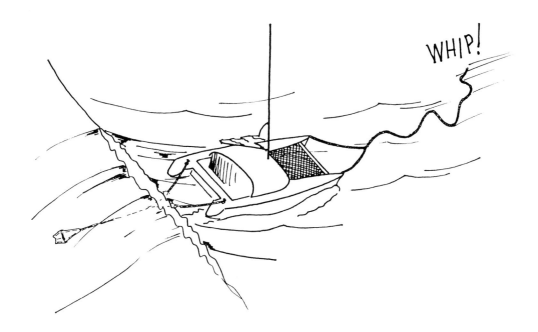

WHIP!

TRAILERING

Know the weight of the multihull and trailer that you are towing. Use a weigh bridge. The towing vehicle should be of approved size and fitted out with a hitch suitable for the load. A multihull on a trailer has high windage for its weight.

Multihull Seamanship Rule:
When trailering watch for strong cross winds.

If in doubt about overhead obstacles then stop and measure them. It is a lot easier than extracting your jammed multihull. Be wary of overhanging trees, low bridges and especially the service stations with low roof lines over the bowsers.

Allow for your mast overhang when cornering. Have the mast end appropriately flagged so as to be visible to following vehicles.

No wonder it came off! You didn't put the safety chains on!

STUCK ON YOU

Remove the trailer jockey wheel before commencing the tow. The towing hitch should be balanced to have approximately 10% of the total tow weight. This can be measured on any portable scale. If the trailer swings from side to side when towing then increase the weight on the hitch. This can be done as easily as moving a fuel tank forward in the hull.

Multihull Seamanship Rule:
Know and measure the overall height and width of your tow.

Prepare the equipment aboard your multihull for the tow. Ensure the rudder is lashed to one side or removed, the rigging wires are all padded to stop rubbing on the hulls and anything lose is stowed away. Lock down any hatches or pop tops. If your tow has fold down beams ensure they cannot open out. Cover hull areas exposed to road mud.

When launching and retrieving always look for overhead power lines. On launching beware of windage effect and have lines ready beforehand.

TRAMPOLINES & SAFETY NETS

Trampolines need care. The material in all trampolines deteriorates in sunlight and use. In tropical areas trampolines may need replacement every two years. If you do not know the age or condition of your trampoline then change it. Cheap insurance.

Multihull Seamanship Rule:
If you think a safety thought - do it.

Falling through a trampoline can, and has, been fatal. Talk to the fish net dealers about ultraviolet resistance. Get a net that will maintain its strength over time. Many netting materials (e.g. nylon and dacron) can be painted to prolong their life. It is a good idea to test your net every now and then; get five athletic people and jump on it when on a safe mooring.

Many nets chafe at securing points. If chafe is bad in one area then redesign the attachment system. You will probably need to stand there during the next gale!

The material of the foredeck trampoline has an effect on the capsize risk if your multihull does a nose dive. If the design is open weave, allowing water to pass, then the tripping effect is greatly reduced. A solid foredeck or tight weave net will contribute to the sudden braking effect.

Netting material can be tied on two ways - with the weave diagonal or straight. When the weave is straight (or 'by the bight') the weave runs parallel with the hulls and cross beams. The best tension is achieved when the net is secured 'by the bight'.

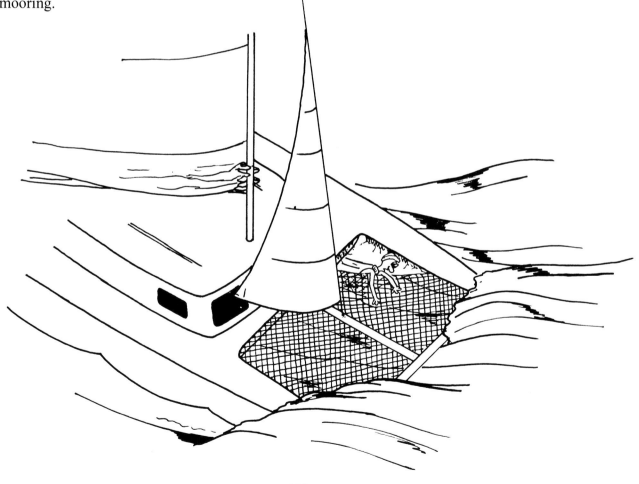

TRANSFERS

Transfer from a capsized or disabled multihull to a ship

Transfer to a ship needs lots of forethought. If the sea state is such that waves backwash from the ship holding station then the transfer should only be attempted if absolutely necessary. There are a number of options. The ship should not come across from windward and drift down on the capsized multihull. It will impact the hull and probably smash it. Crewman on the inverted multihull may well be knocked overboard before nets or line can be attached to them.

If the ship has adequate power to hold position close to the capsized multihull firing a line to the multihull and taking crewman over by harness may work. Ensure a lifejacket is worn and that there is a line tethering back to the multihull. This will allow the rescue line to be retrieved and will also double the security of the person being rescued. Watch for lines being pulled taut and injuring persons on the multihull or being rescued.

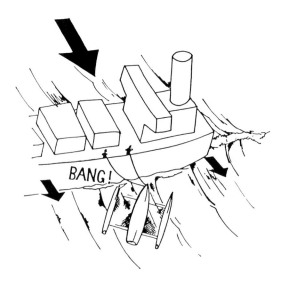

Another option is for the ship to hold station downwind and the person to be rescued drift down via liferaft. The liferaft should remain tethered to the multihull. Nets can be slung over the bow of the ship to enable transfer.

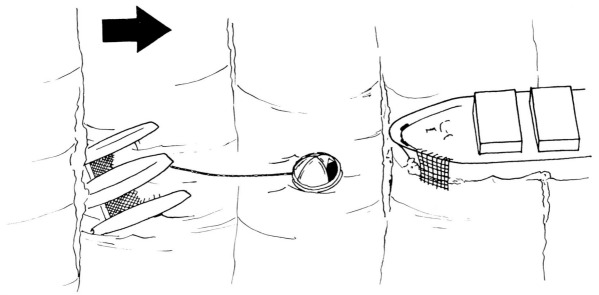

Transfer from a capsized or disabled multihull to a motor vessel

This transfer is basically the same as a ship although the vessel is likely to be able to approach closer. Be aware of sheets, sails and rigging drifting underwater and potentially fouling the propeller.

If the motor vessel has adequate power to hold station it may be able to send a line to the multihull by floating it downwind with a lifejacket or lifering. Avoid the motor vessel approaching the multihull in anything other than calm conditions. This form of direct transfer is the most hazardous to both vessels.

Transfer from a disabled or capsized multihull to another yacht

The biggest problem here is the yacht holding station to affect rescue. One option is for the crew on the capsized multihull to float downwind via a line so that the yacht can approach close-hauled and round up, stopping below the multihull and hooking the crewman out of the water. Only when securely attached to a line from the yacht should any tether to the capsized multihull be released.

Transfer from a capsized multihull to a helicopter

Prepare for this rescue when you see the helicopter. Remove all snags (jury mast, debris) from the deck so that the helicopter can lower the winch line onto the deck for retrieval. In rough seas the helicopter may not be able to hold station over the capsized multihull.

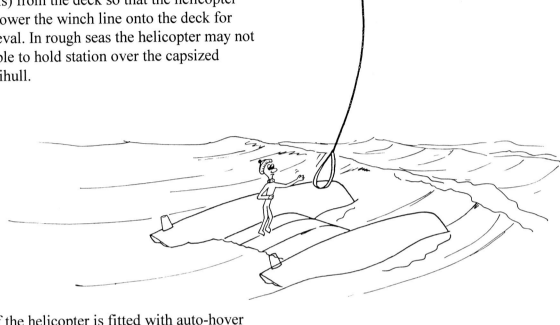

If the helicopter is fitted with auto-hover facility it will need to use the multihull as a reference point. The winch line will be lowered into the water behind the multihull. Crewman should drift back via lifering or liferaft (on a tether) until the winch line is secured to the crewman.

Be aware that when the winch line pulls tight there will be a 'whip' effect. Once secured to the winch line protect your face.

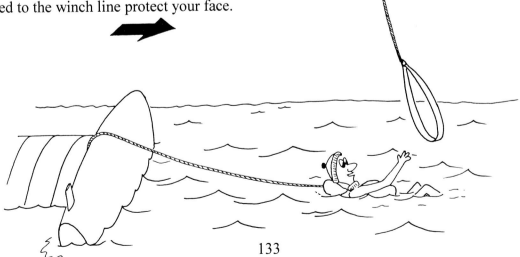

133

Transfer from a disabled multihull to a helicopter

In this situation the mast is a problem. The potential for snagging the winch line is dramatically increased. There are two options. Drop the mast or prepare to enter the water on a tether (wearing a lifejacket) or in a liferaft on a tether and drift downwind behind the multihull. The helicopter can then lower the winch line with safety.

WHALES

Multihulls hit whales. A multihulls shallow draft, lighter construction and speed may be factors involved in whales not being able to detect their approach. Each continent has a fairly predictable whale migratory route and season. For example humpback whales migrate up the east coast of Australia along the edge of the continental shelf in April. Collision usually occurs at night, in rough seas and in poor visibility.

The following can be done to minimise the impact and damage from a whale collision:

• Have centreboards as high as possible and designed to cope with collision

• Fit retracting rudders or impact resistant rudders i.e. able to be grounded

• Avoid whale migratory routes and seasons at night

• Unless racing, sail at a conservative boat speed at night.

GLOSSARY OF MULTIHULL TERMS

Aft: Back, rear or stern of the vessel.

Ama: The outer floats of a trimaran or proa.

Aka: The cross beams connecting the floats of a trimaran to the main hull. Other terms used include crossarms or beams.

Aspect ratio: The height verses the width of a component - usually the mainsail or centreboard(s).

Back: This is forcing wind against a sail to aid manoeuvring. Commonly used when the headsail or jib is backwinded to aid tacking. i.e. The headsail is held on one side while the wind hits it on what is normally the leeward side.

Backwind: See Back.

Backstay: Part of the stay system that supports the mast. The backstay leads to the deck aft of the mast. Some multihulls have permanent backstays, some have none and the mast is supported by sidestays alone. Backstays are sometimes movable. These are called 'Running backstays' and the leeward stay is pulled away from the sails out toward the sidestay. (This stops it rubbing on the sail causing chafe).

Barberhauler: A device of lines and blocks that change where the jib clew is normally held.

Batten: A wood, plastic or fibreglass strip that is inserted into the sail to stiffen the sail and help it hold shape.

Beam: The width of a boat.

Beam reach: A sailing direction where the wind is coming 90 degrees from the centreline.

Bear away: To turn the yacht away from the wind.

Beat: Sailing as close to the wind direction as is possible. As in 'on a beat' or 'beating to windward'. Also called 'close hauled'.

Bilge: The bottom part of the inside of each hull. Usually referred to that area beneath the floorboards or cabin sole.

Bimini: A cockpit cover, usually able to be folded away.

Boom: The spar that supports the bottom (the foot) of the mainsail.

Boom Vang: A device that pulls down the boom to prevent it from lifting. It helps create proper sail shape when the mainsheet it outside the traveller area.

Bow: The forward projection of each hull.

Bowsprit: A pole extending forward of the bow to take the tack of a sail. See Prodder and Spinnaker Pole.

Bridgedeck: The decking area between a catamarans hulls.

Bridle: The arrangement of lines or wires where the pull is taken from two points joining onto a single line. Used when anchoring or when towing a drogue or lying on a parachute sea anchor.

Broach: To swing toward the wind when sailing downwind so that the vessel lies broadside to the waves. Uncommon in multihulls.

Broadside: The side of the hulls. Used as in 'lying broadside' with the hulls sideways to the waves.

Broad Reach: The point of sailing when the wind comes from between the beam (90 degrees) and the wind quartering aft (165 degrees).

Bulkhead: A structural dividing wall in a hull. It may be complete or have access through it to another compartment.

Catamaran: A twin hulled vessel. The hulls are usually identical.

Centre of effort: The theoretical pressure centre of the combined effect of the sails, mast and rigging. This varies as you change sails.

Centre of Lateral Resistance: This is the centre of the sideways force on the underwater section of the vessel. This is the area that stops the vessel sliding sideways.

GLOSSARY OF MULTIHULL TERMS

Centreboard: A board that slides through a slot in the hull to increase lateral resistance. If it is not able to be pivoted it is sometimes called a 'daggerboard'.

Chainplate: A connector attached to the side of the hull to attach the mast rigging onto.

Cleat: A device used to secure a line.

Clew: The corner of a triangular sail closest to the back of the vessel. The corner at the junction of the foot and leech.

Close-hauled: Sailing as close to the wind direction as possible. See Beat.

Close reach: A point of sailing between a beat and a beam reach.

Coachroof: The structure over the saloon of a bridgedeck catamaran.

Cockpit: The area of the deck where steering is usually done and most lines are led to.

Cutter: A rig set up using a single mast, one mainsail and two headsails. The headsails are referred to as the yankee and the staysail.

Daggerboard: See Centreboard.

Displacement: The weight of the water that the vessel replaces when sitting afloat. In common usage it refers to the weight of the boat.

Displacement Hull: A hull designed to pass through the water rather than skim over it.

Downhaul: A line that puts downward load on the luff of a sail. Usually this is at the base of the mast and works on the mainsail.

Downwind: Moving in the same direction as the wind.

Drogue: A device that is towed behind a vessel to slow it down and stabilise its direction. It can be used as emergency steering on multihulls. Made from material, plastic or aluminium.

Eye: Straight into the wind direction. In relation to a cyclone it is the very centre of the circular pattern of weather.

Escape Hatch: A hatch that is set into the multihull to allow access after capsize.

Following Sea: Waves or swell coming from behind the vessel.

Foot: The bottom edge of the sail.

Fore-and-Aft: The length-wise area of the boat.

Foresail: The first working sail in front of the mainsail. Also called a jib.

Forestay: The stay that goes to the front of the vessel from the mast. It usually holds the jib luff or roller furling gear.

Fouled: Caught or tangled.

Furl: Rolling up of a sail and securing it.

Genoa: A large overlapping headsail.

Gooseneck: A device connecting the boom to the mast, capable of swivelling in two directions.

Gull Striker: See Seagull Striker.

Gybe: See Jibe.

Halyard: A line used in the raising or lowering of a sail.

Haul: To pull in with force.

Head: The top corner of a triangular sail.

Header: A wind shift that makes you steer away from your normal course to avoid luffing.

Heading: The direction in which you are sailing or want to sail.

Headsails: Any sails forward of the mast.

Head to Wind: A yachts position when the bows are pointing into the wind.

Heel: The amount the vessel is leaning over due to the wind.

Helm: The steering device or position. As in 'At the Helm.'

Hounds: The mast fitting to which the forestay fitting is attached.

Hove-to: A position where the yacht is nearly stationary and the bows pointed slightly toward the wind.

Irons: A position where the sailboat is not moving and pointing directly into the wind. Called 'In irons'.

GLOSSARY OF MULTIHULL TERMS

Jib: A triangular sail attached to the forestay and forward of the mainmast.

Jibe: Turning the boat downwind from one direction to another with the back of the boat passing through the wind direction. Also spelt gybe.

Jury-Rig: A rig made for temporary or emergency use.

Keel: The lower edge of a vessel under the water.

Ketch: Main mast forward, smaller mast aft.

Kite: See Spinnaker.

Knot: One nautical mile per hour. A nautical mile is slightly longer than a statute mile.

Lateral Resistance: The force that stops the hull from sliding sideways in the water.

Leech: The back edge of a sail.

Lee: The side of an object shaded or in a different direction from the wind.

Lee helm: A tendency to sail away from the wind direction when the steering is released. It is due to an imbalance between the centre of lateral resistance and the centre of effort.

Lee Shore: The shoreline that is downwind.

Leeward: See Lee.

Leeway: The amount the vessel is pushed sideways by the wind.

Luff: The front edge of the sail. It also means the effect on a sail when the wind no longer fills the sail and starts to ease pressure on the sail.

Masthead: The top of the mast.

Multihull: A vessel of two or more hulls.

Nacelle: The central area of a catamaran where the bridge deck is lowered to support a motor.

Parachute anchor: A parachute that is used in the water to stop wind drift. A sea anchor.

Pitching: A rocking fore-and-aft motion.

Pitchpole: Capsizing a boat stern over bow.

Planing Hull: A hull designed to skim over the water.

Pointing: Sailing toward the wind direction as high as possible.

Port: The left side of a vessel when facing the bow. Also used to describe a place where vessels dock.

Port Tack: A point of sailing where the wind is coming from the port side.

Pounding: The striking action of waves under the hull.

Preventer: A line or block and tackle that is used to secure the boom out the side of the yacht - to 'prevent' accidental gybing.

Proa: A two-hulled vessel that has one hull smaller than the other.

Prodder: A permanently attached pole that extends from the bow to hold the tack of a sail (usually a reacher or spinnaker).

Rake: The inclination of the mast away from straight up and down.

Reach: To sail with the true wind at approximately 90 degrees to the direction of sailing. The direction of sailing between a beat and running. Usually broken up into a 'close reach', a 'beam reach' or a 'broad reach'.

Reef: To reduce the area of the sails.

Rig: The mast, stays and sail plan.

Rigging: The ropes, wires and cable that support the mast.

Roach: The area of a sail that extends behind an imaginary line from the clew to the head.

Rode: A rope line that has some elasticity used for anchoring, running a drogue or lying to a parachute.

Roller Furling: A storage sail device which rolls the sail around to attachment points.

Roller Reefing: A device to make the sail smaller to match wind conditions by wrapping the sail around either the boom, forestay or into a wire in the mast.

Round Up: To turn the boat into the direction of the wind.

GLOSSARY OF MULTIHULL TERMS

Run: To sail with the wind coming from behind the yacht. To sail downwind.

Running backstay: See Backstay.

Running Rigging: The control cables for the mast, spars and sails.

Seagull Striker: An arrangement of wire to counteract the upward pull of the forestay on the forebeam of a catamaran. Also called a Gull Striker.

Sheets: The lines used to control the sails.

Shrouds: The stays that support the mast on either side.

Sidestays: Supporting wires of the mast that lead to the side of the multihull - usually just behind the level of the mast.

Skeg: An attachment to the keel at the back of the vessel to protect or secure the rudder.

Sloop: A single headsail rig where the forestay goes to the top of the mast.

Spinnaker: A light, ballooning-type headsail that is used when sailing downwind. Various shapes ranging from symmetrical straight downwind type to asymmetrical 'reaching' types.

Spinnaker Pole: A removable pole that is mounted on the mast to hold the spinnaker tack. Rarely used on multihulls because the clew can be triangulated and held due to the vessels beam by lines alone. See Prodder.

Stall: The slowing effect on boat speed when the sails are pulled in too tight in relation to the wind direction.

Starboard: The right side of the boat when facing the bow.

Starboard tack:. A point of sailing where the wind is coming over the starboard side.

Stay: A wire rope used to support the mast.

Staysail: The back or aft sail of a double headsail rig.

Stern: The back (aft) end of the boat.

Surf: To sail on the front of a wave.

Tack: (1) The front bottom corner of a sail. (2) To change direction by turning the bow through the direction of the wind so that the wind is coming over the other side of the boat.

Targa Bar: An inverted 'U' shaped beam that is raised off the back beam for the purpose of supporting solar panels, aerials, dinghy lifting tackle and occasionally the mainsheet track and blocks.

Telltale: A piece of material or ribbon attached to sails or shrouds that helps determine wind direction and sail trim.

Tiller: A steering handle linked to the rudder(s).

Topping Lift: A line that supports the boom by its outer end. Used when the mainsail is not raised.

Trampoline: A netted area filling in a space between hulls and beams.

Traveller: The device that slides along and controls the mainsail position from the centreline.

Trimaran: A three hulled vessel.

Warps: Lines used to tie the yacht to the quayside or marina.

Weather: The term indicates which side the wind is on. As in 'to weather'.

Weather Helm: The tendency for the vessel to turn into the wind when the steering is released. It is caused by an inbalance between the centre of effort and the centre of lateral resistance. The centre of effort is behind the centre of lateral resistance in this case.

Windward: Toward the wind.

Wing Mast: A rotating aerofoil-shaped mast with a large surface area fore-and-aft that adds to the total sail area.

Yankee: The forward sail of a double headsail rig.

Yaw: To swing off course from side to side.

INDEX